COMPREHENSIVE RESEARCH
AND STUDY GUIDE

Robert Frost

BLOOM'S
MAJOR
POETS

EDITED AND WITH AN INTRODUCTION
BY HAROLD BLOOM

CURRENTLY AVAILABLE

BLOOM'S MAJOR WORLD POETS

Geoffrey Chaucer

Emily Dickinson

John Donne

T. S. Eliot

Robert Frost

Langston Hughes

John Milton

Edgar Allan Poe

Shakespeare's Poems & Sonnets

Alfred, Lord Tennyson

Walt Whitman

William Wordsworth

BLOOM'S MAJOR SHORT STORY WRITERS

William Faulkner

F. Scott Fitzgerald

Ernest Hemingway

O. Henry

James Joyce

Herman Melville

Flannery O'Connor

Edgar Allan Poe

J. D. Salinger

John Steinbeck

Mark Twain

Eudora Welty

Robert Frost

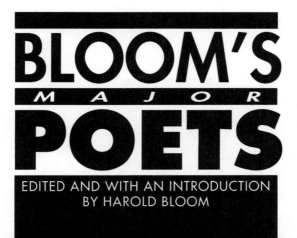

BLOOM'S *MAJOR* POETS

EDITED AND WITH AN INTRODUCTION
BY HAROLD BLOOM

 3 5 7 9 8 6 4 2

Library of Congress Cataloging-in-Publication Data

Robert Frost / edited and with an introduction by Harold Bloom.
p.   cm.—(Bloom's major poets)
Includes bibliographical references and index.
ISBN: 0-7910-5105-6
1. Frost, Robert, 1874–1963—Criticism and interpretation.
I. Bloom, Harold.   II. Series.
PS3511.R94Z9159   1998
811'.52—dc21
98-35358
CIP

Chelsea House Publishers
1974 Sproul Road, Suite 400
Broomall, PA 19008-0914

Contributing Editor: Barbara Fischer

Contents

User's Guide

This volume is designed to present biographical, critical, and bibliographical information on the author's best-known or most important poems. Following Harold Bloom's editor's note and introduction are a detailed biography of the author, discussing major life events and important literary accomplishments. A thematic and structural analysis of each poem follows, tracing significant themes, patterns, and motifs in the work.

A selection of critical extracts, derived from previously published material from leading critics, analyzes aspects of each poem. The extracts consist of statements from the author, if available, early reviews of the work, and later evaluations up to the present. A bibliography of the author's writings (including a complete list of all books written, cowritten, edited, and translated), a list of additional books and articles on the author and the work, and an index of themes and ideas in the author's writings conclude the volume.

～

Harold Bloom is Sterling Professor of the Humanities at Yale University and Henry W. and Albert A. Berg Professor of English at the New York University Graduate School. He is the author of over 20 books and the editor of more than 30 anthologies of literary criticism.

Professor Bloom's works include *Shelley's Mythmaking* (1959), *The Visionary Company* (1961), *Blake's Apocalypse* (1963), *Yeats* (1970), *A Map of Misreading* (1975), *Kabbalah and Criticism* (1975), and *Agon: Toward a Theory of Revisionism* (1982). *The Anxiety of Influence* (1973) sets forth Professor Bloom's provocative theory of the literary relationships between the great writers and their predecessors. His most recent books include *The American Religion* (1992), *The Western Canon* (1994), *Omens of Millennium: The Gnosis of Angels, Dreams, and Resurrection* (1996), and *Shakespeare: The Invention of the Human*, 1998.

Professor Bloom earned his Ph.D. from Yale University in 1955 and has served on the Yale faculty since then. He is a 1985 MacArthur Foundation Award recipient and served as the Charles Eliot Norton Professor of Poetry at Harvard University in 1987–88. He is currently the editor of other Chelsea House series in literary criticism, including BLOOM'S NOTES, BLOOM'S MAJOR SHORT STORY WRITERS, MAJOR LITERARY CHARACTERS, MODERN CRITICAL VIEWS, MODERN CRITICAL INTERPRETATIONS, and WOMEN WRITERS OF ENGLISH AND THEIR WORKS.

Editor's Note

The criticism afforded to Robert Frost has been of a rather high quality, as most of the views excerpted in this volume will demonstrate. Nine of Frost's best poems are discussed, and I will note only some high points here. Richard Poirier, anticipating his own later Pragmatism, teaches us to distrust Frost's devotion to "home" in "Death of the Hired Man," while Katherine Kearns, from a somewhat feminist perspective, also persuades us that the poem's vision of marital harmony is open to the reader's suspicion.

Frost's rather enigmatic pastoralism, with its dialectical views of nature, is analyzed by John F. Lynen and George F. Bagby in ways that differ, yet illuminate one another.

"Directive," an immensely challenging poem, receives distinguished responses from Marie Borroff, Sydney Lea, Herbert Marks, and Charles Berger. Where Borroff centers upon Frost's crucial allusion to the Gospel of Mark, Lea distinguishes Frost's deliberately wrought mock-sublime from Wordsworth's more assured sublimity. Marks and Berger both outline, with considerable brilliance, Frost's riddling paradoxes in regard to memory and its limitations.

Introduction

HAROLD BLOOM

Robert Frost is one of the major American poets, equal in eminence to Ralph Waldo Emerson, Walt Whitman, and Emily Dickinson in the Nineteenth century, and to T. S. Eliot, Wallace Stevens, and Hart Crane in the Twentieth. Of his peers, Frost shares most with Emerson, whose meditations in *The Condition of Life* are particularly Frostian:

> We cannot write the order of the variable winds. How can we penetrate the law of our shifting moods and susceptibility? Yet they differ as all and nothing. Instead of the firmament of yesterday, which our eyes require, it is to-day an eggshell which coops us in; we cannot even see what or where our stars of destiny are. From day to day, the capital facts of human life are hidden from our eyes. Suddenly the mist rolls up, and reveals them, and we think how much good time is gone, that might have been saved, had any hint of these things been shown. A sudden rise in the road shows us the system of mountains, and we are parties to our various fortune. If life seems a succession of dreams, yet poetic justice is done in dreams also. The visions of good men are good; it is the undisciplined will that is whipped with bad thoughts and bad fortunes. When we break laws, we lose our hold on the central reality. Like sick men in hospitals, we change only from bed to bed, from one folly to another; and it cannot signify much what becomes of such castaways,—wailing, stupid, comatose—lifted from bed to bed, from the nothing of life to the nothing of death.

This is from the essay "Illusions," and could be an epigraph to all of Frost's poetry. Emerson may now be the most undervalued of all our major poets, never by Frost, who wrote that the sage of Concord's "Uriel" was "the greatest Western poem yet." Certainly the doctrine of Emerson's Uriel is the purest Frost:

> "Line in nature is not found,
> Unit and universe are round;
> In vain produce, all rays return;
> Evil will bless, and ice will burn."

This Emersonian spiritual ferocity always remained Frost's. It is there in the early "The Trial By Existence" (from *A Boy's Will*, 1913) and abides still in "A Cabin in the Clearing" (from *In the Clearing*, 1962). Valor reigns, though existence strips us of pride, and we end in pain and mystification. That is the argument of "The Trial by Existence," and prevails in "A Cabin in the Clearing," where all of us "are too sudden to be credible." Poems, being momentary stays against confusion, are also too sudden to be credible.

Frost's most famous poems may be "The Road Not Taken" and "Stopping by Woods on a Snowy Evening." They owe their popularity to a palpable exquisiteness, but probably are misread by most of their public. Frost remarked of "The Road Not Taken" that: "It's a tricky poem, very tricky," while "Stopping by Woods on a Snowy Evening" is a rather dangerous poem, tempting the poet (and the reader) with a freedom that would also be destruction. So tricky is "The Road Not Taken" that the alternate routes are presented as though there were no pragmatic difference between them, and yet taking the one supposedly less traveled by has made a total difference in the speaker's life. As allegory or irony, this is open-ended: was it a choice of the poetic vocation, or of one woman rather than another? The final stanza, too sudden to be credible, is overtly the least trustworthy in the poem.

"Stopping by Woods on a Snowy Evening" (to me the superior poem) teases us with a near-nihilism, and then reaccepts the world of continuities and obligations, whose emblem is the tingle of harness bells. Tempted by the dark loneliness of deep woods, speaker and reader share in the easy sweep of the wind and snow fall, intimating a solitary quest, where there can be no promises. When Frost observed that a poem was a momentary stay against confusion, he slyly played upon the finer edges of the word "confusion," as he did again in his late poem "Directive" (to me his best), where the traveler, having reached his waters and watering place, is commanded to "Drink and be whole again beyond confusion." Frost's "confusion" is inherited from Emerson's "Uriel," where the heavens come apart after Uriel's rhapsodic affirmation that "Evil will bless, and ice will burn":

> The balance-beam of Fate was bent;
> The bounds of good and ill were rent;
> Strong Hades could not keep his own,
> But all slid to confusion.

Both students of language, Emerson and Frost seem to have known that the Indo-European root of "confusion" originally signified the pouring of a libation to the gods. To be whole again beyond confusion is to have transcended such worship. Frost's poetic religion, like Emerson's, was *Self*-Reliance, a lonely doctrine:

> That thought, by what I can now nearest approach to say it, is this. When good is near you, when you have life in yourself, it is not by any known or accustomed way; you shall not discern the footprints of any other; you shall not hear any name;—the way, the thought, the good, shall be wholly strange and new.

This Emersonian insistence upon unprecendentedness was Frost's poetic gospel. Formally, Frost remained a traditionalist, totally unaffected by Emerson's greatest disciple, Walt Whitman. But the poetic argument of Frost's work, in "Directive," "The Oven Bird," "Design," "Birches," and so many other triumphs, is extraordinarily individual. Frost was a severe poet, savage and original in his primal vision, and as much an Emersonial fulfillment as Whitman had been, or as Wallace Stevens and Hart Crane proved to be, in Frost's own era. ❀

Biography of
Robert Frost

(1874–1963)

Poet Robert Lee Frost was born on March 26, 1874, in San Francisco, California, to Isabelle Moodie Frost and William Prescott Frost. William Frost, a Harvard-educated journalist, worked for the San Francisco *Daily Evening Post* and was elected a delegate to the Democratic National Convention in 1880. His poor health, violence, drinking, and gambling upset any possibility of family stability. Isabelle Frost, the daughter of a Scottish sea captain, moved to the United States at age 12. She was a follower of the Swedenborgian religion and instructed Frost in its beliefs. Frost received much of his early education at home, and his mother often read aloud from the works of Shakespeare, Poe, Emerson, and Wordsworth, as well as others.

After his father's death from tuberculosis in 1885, Frost moved with his mother and sister to New England, where they settled in Lawrence, Massachusetts. Attending Lawrence High School, Frost published several poems in the school magazine and was named class poet. He also played right end on the school's football team. He graduated in 1892, sharing valedictorian honors with Elinor White, to whom he became engaged.

Though he passed Harvard's entrance exams, Frost lacked the money needed to attend the school. He instead attended Dartmouth College, but left after less than a semester, and pursued a variety of jobs, including teaching at his mother's private school and working in a textile mill. In 1894 he published a few poems in *The Independent* and began corresponding with its literary editor, Susan Hayes Ward. He tried to persuade Elinor to leave St. Lawrence University and marry him, but she was determined to complete her degree. On one occasion, he presented her with *Twilight*, a collection of five of his poems, but she responded coolly and he set off on a despairing excursion south through New York to the Dismal Swamp of Virginia and North Carolina.

He married Elinor in December of 1895. In the early years of their marriage, Frost attended Harvard as a special student but withdrew in 1899 and took up poultry farming to support his growing family. The Frosts' family life, often strained by emotional and financial anxieties, was marked by a series of tragedies. Their first child, Elliott, died of cholera at age three. Another child, Elinor Bettina, died two days after birth. Of the four children who lived to adulthood, Frost's daughter Marjorie died of childbed fever at age 29, and his son Carol committed suicide at age 38. Another daughter, Irma, had to be institutionalized for mental illness, as did Frost's sister Jeanie.

In the busy years of family responsibilities between 1900 and 1912, Frost pursued farming and teaching, trying to fit in time to write poetry, often at night at the kitchen table. Living on a 30-acre farm in Derry, New Hampshire, Frost published stories and articles in the *Eastern Poultryman*. He visited New York City in 1903 in an attempt to interest several editors in his poetry, but was unsuccessful. Pressed for money and frustrated by his farming efforts, Frost taught for several years at the Pinkerton Academy in Derry, New Hampshire. He eventually moved his family off the farm, and later accepted a position teaching at State Normal School in Plymouth.

In 1912, Frost moved with his wife and four children to England to concentrate on poetry and book publication. *A Boy's Will* was published by the London firm of David Nutt and Company in 1913, and was reviewed favorably by American poet and critic Ezra Pound (1885–1972), a highly influential figure in modernist letters. Nutt published *North of Boston* a year later. While in England, Frost made Pound's acquaintance and also met poet and essayist Edward Thomas (1878–1917) and other important literary figures of the time. When he returned to the United States after two-and-a-half years abroad, *North of Boston* was published in New York by Henry Holt and widely acclaimed, selling a phenomenal 20,000 copies. Frost was almost immediately famous.

Several important and well-received books followed in rapid succession. Continuing to write poetry, Frost began to pursue what would be a lifelong career as a part-time college teacher and poet-in-residence, moving with his family between teaching posts and farms in Franconia, New Hampshire, and South Shaftsbury, Vermont. He held positions at many colleges, including the University of Michigan, Dartmouth, Harvard, and, for extended periods, Amherst.

In the course of his lifetime, Frost was recognized with more than 17 honorary degrees from prestigious colleges and universities in the United States and England. He continued to write books of poetry, receiving the Pulitzer Prize an unprecedented four times, for *New Hampshire* (1924), *Collected Poems* (1931), *A Further Range* (1937), and *A Witness Tree* (1943).

Late in life, Frost led a career as a cultural emissary and public personage, touring South America, Europe, and the Middle East. He was named Consultant in Poetry to the Library of Congress in 1958 (the position that is currently known as Poet Laureate). In 1961 he read "The Gift Outright" at President Kennedy's inauguration. In 1962, in a much-publicized tour of the Soviet Union, he met and conversed privately with Premier Khrushchev. His 75th and 85th birthdays were recognized by commendations from the U.S. Senate.

Despite his great popularity, Frost was often a dissatisfied and troubled man, suffering from periods of depression. His marriage to Elinor was one of strong mutual devotion but was also deeply and even bitterly contentious. Frost has been criticized for bigotry, authoritarianism, jealousy, and even cruelty in both his private and public life. He was outspoken about his opposition to the New Deal and left-wing politics, and he alienated many members of the literary establishment. Feeling that he was not valued as highly as modernist writers such as Pound and T. S. Eliot (1888–1964), he frequently jockeyed for compensation and recognition, and complained that he did not receive the Nobel Prize.*

When Frost died on January 29, 1963, at the age of 88, he was the most popular and famous American poet of the century, a cultural icon, and an esteemed literary figure of great influence. Critical attention continues to be devoted to the skill and power of his poetry. ❀

*Mordecai Marcus, *The Poems of Robert Frost: An Explication* (Boston: G. K. Hall & Co., 1991), 8–9. See also Frost's authorized biography by Lawrence Thompson, and a more recent biography by Jeffrey Meyers (Boston: Houghton Mifflin, 1996).

Thematic Analysis of
"The Death of the Hired Man"
(including a discussion of "Mending Wall")

"The Death of the Hired Man" is the first of several narrative poems in *North of Boston* (1914), Frost's second book. These poems, set in rural New England, present speakers who are grappling with situations that are at once commonplace and marked by extraordinary severity and power. Frost innovatively uses dialogue written in blank verse (unrhymed iambic pentameter) to advance dramatic situations. The dialogue has a vernacular fluidity, immediacy, and seamlessness that suggest we are overhearing an actual conversation, an effect Frost achieves only through precise modulations of phrasing and diction. Some reviewers claim that Frost would have been better off writing prose fiction, but this judgment overlooks his striking poetic achievement in grafting common idiomatic speech onto a traditional metrical pattern.

The poem begins with Mary, a country housewife, waiting for the evening return of her husband, Warren. When he arrives, she leads him out to the porch steps and tells him that Silas, an aging itinerant farmhand, has returned to their farm in search of work. Warren had previously dismissed Silas from his employ for his unreliability. Silas tended to leave their farm in haying time, when he was most needed, because he could find higher wages elsewhere, only to show up again in winter looking for odd jobs. He has exhausted Warren's patience.

The discussion turns to matters of compassion and obligation, as Mary and Warren examine the nature of Silas's loyalty and how far their loyalty to him should extend. Mary explains that she found Silas earlier in the day, haggard and asleep by the barn, and brought him to the house to revive, where he carried on a "jumbled" conversation with her. Silas, preoccupied with an argument he remembered having four summers ago with a college student, Harold Wilson, insists, implausibly, that he and Harold can work together again on Mary's and Warren's farm.

As she relates Silas's uneasiness about Harold's book learning and his need to promote his own knowledge as valuable, Mary reminds Warren of Silas's skill at building a load of hay. Warren acknowledges this ability as marking Silas's usefulness, his one "marketable" skill in this economy of agricultural life. Mary pities Silas for having only this skill to forge a tenuous link between himself and others, and rather sentimentally concludes that Silas has neither memories to recall with pride nor hope for a future. The conversation pauses, and Frost turns our attention to an image of the external world, the moon in the western sky. Mary is figured as part of nature, tenderly and sensuously embracing the moonlight in her lap. She allows Warren time to think, then tells him that Silas "has come home to die."

Warren focuses the conversation abruptly on the word "home" and its meaning. By considering Silas's family history and what is to be done with him, Mary and Warren weigh, in a carefully nuanced dialogue, the subtleties of our understanding of human responsibility, kinship, and justice. More than simply drawing a picture of the "local color" of this rural community, Frost uses the dialogue to examine the social and familial fabric of a place where interaction with neighbors punctuates a potentially unbearable sense of isolation. Warren insists that Silas should go to his wealthy brother's home, 13 miles away. Mary observes that the wandering and even dissolute Silas might be too prideful to turn to his "successful" brother, and urges Warren to "be kind" and indulge Silas's offer of work. Warren enters the house while Mary remains outside watching the moon; he returns a moment later with the news that Silas is dead.

The narrative encompasses a very brief period of time in which little action occurs, but in it we get a complex characterization of both Mary and Warren and a portrait of their marriage. Mary's perspective of compassionate identification and emotional response contrasts Warren's more rational view of fair judgment. Frost encapsulates Mary's attitude in one present tense, active sentence, "I sympathize," and strengthens our sense of Mary's sensitivity and perceptive acuity with the mention of simple bodily gestures. Mary listened closely for the sound of Warren's footsteps that indicate his approach, then "ran on tiptoe" down the hall to greet him, a movement that conveys both the tentativeness and the assuredness of her proactive decision to "put him on his guard." Her gesture of lightly strumming the "morning-glory strings" shows her patience and the sense of continuity and harmony she has with nature. Warren's seemingly insignificant gestures underscore his characterization as well. When he picks up and breaks a stick, he demonstrates his frustration and reluctance to compromise, as well as his wish for decisive clarity about the situation.

Differences in the way Mary and Warren employ and decline to employ language also characterize their modes of thinking and reacting. As does "Home Burial," another dialogue poem in *New Hampshire* that vividly evokes a marital relationship, "The Death of the Hired Man" examines the communicative strain between men and women, but it offers a far more balanced view of domestic give and take. Mary is aware that her silences speak as much as her words do, touching the morning glories "As if she played unheard some tenderness/That wrought on him beside her in the night." This intimate communication contrasts Warren's more sarcastic concession to her persuasiveness. With somewhat caustic wit, he remembers Harold's and Silas's bickering and his response to it: "Yes, I took care to keep well out of earshot." His mode of communication permits him to keep his distance. When he quips, "Home is the place where, when you have to go there,/They have to take you in," he sharply emphasizes the negative, compulsory side of the humane obligation Mary propounds.

Warren's definition of home offers an example of Frost's memorable and witty statements of familiar feelings. But Frost implies that condensed and pithy expressions cut several ways: they "ring true," but they also acknowledge the necessarily approximate and "not-quite-right"-ness of language. Mary expresses this difficulty when she says, "I know just how it feels/To think of the right thing to say too late." Her expression is itself a perfectly condensed statement—a statement about the very inability to make such statements when emotional urgency demands them.

In the discussion of Silas's debate with Harold Wilson, Frost brings to light several other sets of potentially conflicting attitudes, contrasting youth and age, formal education and folk wisdom, worldly values and "common sense." Though Silas can scoff at Harold's desire to learn Latin and the violin, he is still disturbed by the discrepancy between Harold's values and his own. Mary observes that "those days trouble Silas like a dream," suggesting that Silas continues to grapple with a haunting but irrecoverable past, and also that the gap between Harold's and Silas's systems of value is as uncrossable as consciousness and dreaming. Harold's "assurance piqued him," and Silas rebuts by proposing, as a counterexample to "book-learning," the ability to "find water with a hazel prong," a reference to divining, an ancient practice based on intuition, not scientific reasoning. In Warren's observation that "You never see him [Silas] standing on the hay/He's trying to lift, straining to lift himself," Frost suggests the merits of the hired man's facility with the world around him, free from self-involved intellectual anxieties. Nonetheless, Frost does not come down unequivocally on the side of either set of values.

Frost masterfully uses small details to set the scene and its mood. Through images that faintly suggest a strange uneasiness, Frost modulates the tone and forebodes the final realization of Silas's death. From the first line, with Mary "musing on the lamp-flame," the reader is given a sense of Mary's attentiveness. Always attuned to the physical world, she observes that Silas is "changed," and then that "he made me feel so queer," giving us a vague symptomatology of his ailing condition that foreshadows the end. The most excruciating detail of the poem is seeing Silas roll "his old head on that sharp-edged chair back." Though a simple and innocuous movement, the image hones the pathos of the poem and suggests that an impending crisis will sever Silas' s hold on the world.

When, in the poem's final movement, Mary watches to see if a cloud will "hit" the moon, the matter-of-fact observation has an insouciance as well as an almost sinister weight, suggesting the inevitability of fate and forces beyond human control. Warren returns and pronounces Silas's fate in one indisputable monosyl-lable, "dead," and we are left with a sense that it could not have been otherwise. The speakers, and the poem, are silenced. "Dead" is, after all, the "last word"—the last word spoken in this poem, and the last word of any life.

"Mending Wall," one of Frost's most analyzed poems, immediately precedes "The Death of the Hired Man" in North of Boston, setting up thematic and formal concerns that are explored and contrasted in the narrative poems that follow. It, too, presents farm work and the relations of neighbors in a rural community, relations that take on metaphorical significances—the meditation in "Mending Wall" exceeds the literal circumstances that occasion it. The speaker muses that "something there is that doesn't love a wall." That "something" is more than just the harsh weather that creates gaps in stone walls, more also than some imagined mischievous presence of "elves":

Frost identifies a deep human resistance to formal principles more generally, a reluctance to erect obstacles to freedom, and a desire to see barriers break down. On the other hand, the neighbor's insistence that "good fences make good neighbors" poses the counterdesire to keep boundaries firmly in place, to demarcate what is "yours" and "mine" and preserve the clear confines that circumscribe expectations. Even though the two farms have no real need for a wall between their respective orchards, the neighbor persists in a customary practice that asserts an explicitly paternal tradition.

The tension between these two views of "walls"—resistance to formal principles and tacit conformation to upholding them—operates throughout *North of Boston* as well as much of Frost's later poetry. Like Mary and Warren and these two fence-building neighbors, pairs of speakers in Frost's poetry often face each other across different kinds of walls, distances, and gulfs—reaching various kinds of mediations and compromises between them. ❁

Critical Views on
"The Death of the Hired Man"

EZRA POUND ON *NORTH OF BOSTON*'S RECEPTION

[Ezra Pound (1885–1972), American poet, translator, and literary critic, was a central figure in modernism in English and American literature. He was the leader of the early Imagists, the influential founding editor of several magazines in the 1910s and 1920s, and the promoter of writers including T. S. Eliot (1888–1964), James Joyce (1882–1941), and Frost. His books of poetry include *Personae* (1909), *Hugh Selwyn Mauberly* (1920), and *The Cantos* (1930–1970). Among his critical works are *ABC of Reading* (1934) and *Literary Essays* (1954). In this review of *North of Boston,* Pound addresses Frost's need to go abroad for publication and compares his work to the poetry American editors were typically publishing at the time.]

It is a sinister thing that so American, I might even say so parochial, a talent as that of Robert Frost should have to be exported before it can find due encouragement and recognition.

Even Emerson had sufficient elasticity of mind to find something in the "yawp." One doesn't need to like a book or a poem or a picture in order to recognize artistic vigor. But the typical American editor of the last twenty years has resolutely shut his mind against serious American writing. I do not exaggerate, I quote exactly, when I say that these gentlemen deliberately write to authors that such and such a matter is "too unfamiliar to our readers."

There was once an American editor who would even print me, so I showed him Frost's *Death of the Hired Man.* He wouldn't have it; he had printed a weak pseudo-Masefieldian poem about a hired man two months before, one written in a stilted pseudo-literary language, with all sorts of floridities and worn-out ornaments.

Mr. Frost is an honest writer, writing from himself, from his own knowledge and emotion; not simply picking up the manner which magazines are accepting at the moment, and applying it to topics in vogue. He is quite consciously and definitely putting New England rural life into verse. He is not using themes that anybody could have cribbed out of Ovid.

There are only two passions in art; there are only love and hate—with endless modifications. Frost has been honestly fond of the New England people, I dare say with spells of irritation. He has given their life honestly and seriously. He has never turned aside to make fun of it. He has taken their tragedy as tragedy, their stubbornness as stubbornness. I know more of farm life than I did before I had read his poems. That means I know more of "Life."

Mr. Frost has dared to write, and for the most part with success, in the natural speech of New England; in natural spoken speech, which is very different from the "natural" speech of the newspapers, and of many professors. His poetry is a bit slow, but you aren't held up every five minutes by the feeling that you are listening to a fool; so perhaps you read it just as easily and quickly as you might read the verse of some of the sillier and more "vivacious" writers.

—Ezra Pound, "Review of North of Boston," *Poetry* 5, No. 3 (December 1914): 127–28

⚘

AMY LOWELL ON *NORTH OF BOSTON* AND ITS PORTRAIT OF NEW ENGLAND

[Amy Lowell (1874–1925), American critic and leading poet of the Imagist school, was known for her bold experimentation and alliances with radical schools of poetry. She is the author of several books of poetry and criticism, including *Tendencies in Modern American Poetry* (1917). In this review, she discusses how Frost uniquely captures New England life.]

Indeed, Mr. Frost is only expatriated in a physical sense. Living in England he is, nevertheless, saturated with New England. For not only is his work New England in subject, it is so in technique. No hint of European forms has crept into it. It is certainly the most American volume of poetry which has appeared for some time. I use the word

"American" in the way it is constantly employed by contemporary reviewers, to mean work of a color so local to be almost photographic. Mr. Frost's book is American in the sense that Whittier is American, and not at all in that subtler sense in which Poe ranks as the greatest American poet.

The thing which makes Mr. Frost's work remarkable is the fact that he has chosen to write it as verse. We have been flooded for twenty years with New England stories in prose. The finest and most discerning are the little masterpieces of Alice Brown. She too is a poet in her descriptions, she too has caught the desolation and "dourness" of lonely New England farms, but unlike Mr. Frost she has a rare sense of humor, and that, too, is of New England, although no hint of it appears in *North of Boston*. And just because of the lack of it, just because its place is taken by an irony, sardonic and grim, Mr. Frost's book reveals a disease which is eating into the vitals of our New England life, at least in its rural communities.

What is there in the hard, vigorous climate of these states which plants the seeds of degeneration? Is the violence and ugliness of their religious belief the cause of these twisted and tortured lives? Have the sane, full-blooded men all been drafted away to the cities, or the West, leaving behind only feeble remainders of a once fine stock? The question again demands an answer after the reading of Mr. Frost's book. [...]

Mr. Frost has reproduced both people and scenery with a vividness which is extraordinary. Here are the huge hills, undraped by any sympathetic legend, felt as things hard and unyielding, almost sinister, not exactly feared, but regarded as in some sort influences nevertheless. Here are great stretches of blueberry pasture lying in the sun; and again, autumn orchards cracking with fruit which it is almost too much trouble to gather. Heavy thunderstorms drench the lonely roads and spatter on the walls of farm-houses rotting in abandonment; and the modern New England town, with narrow frame houses, visited by drummers alone, is painted in all its ugliness. For Mr. Frost's is not the kindly New England of Whittier, nor the humorous and sensible one of [James Russell] Lowell; it is a latter-day New England, where a civilization is decaying to give place to another and very different one.

—Amy Lowell, "North of Boston," *New Republic 2* (February 20, 1915), p. 81

Denis Donoghue on Frost and Social Darwinism

[Denis Donoghue is a professor of English and American Letters at New York University. His numerous works of criticism include *Connoisseurs of Chaos* (1965), *Ferocious Alphabets* (1981), and *Being Modern Together* (1991), as well as books on William Butler Yeats, Emily Dickinson, and Walter Pater. In this extract, Donoghue examines Frost's relation to the theories of Social Darwinism, in light of which "The Death of the Hired Man" and "Mending Wall" might be interpreted as taking a view of "evolution and dissolution."]

If we look for such a structure [of conviction] in the America of Frost's youth, we find it—I shall argue—in the ideas of the Social Darwinists, especially in men like Herbert Spencer and William Graham Sumner and other voices that clamored in America from the 1870s up to the end of the century.

To support this it is necessary to bring the leading tenets of the Social Darwinists together, at least in rough paraphrase, and to show their presence in a number of Frost's poems. The basic idea is that the natural world is a competitive situation in which the best competitors will win. Hence it follows that those who win are the best, and therefore the fittest to survive. Herbert Spencer believed that the pressure of subsistence upon population is bound to have a good effect on the human race. In any event, the whole effort of nature is to get rid of the weak, the unfit. "If they are sufficiently complete to live, they *do* live, and it is well they should live. If they are not sufficiently complete to live, they die, and it is best they should die." Hence the only feasible ethical standard is the right of every man to do as he pleases, subject only to the condition that he does not infringe upon the equal rights of others. (This is why good fences make good neighbors.) There is also the idea of the conservation of energy, or—as Spencer preferred to call it—the persistence of force. "Everywhere in the universe man observes the incessant redistribution of matter and motion, rhythmically apportioned between evolution and dissolution. Evolution is the progressive integration of matter, accompanied by dissipation of motion; dissolution is the disorganization of matter accompanied by the absorption of motion." Hence Spencer inferred that anything that is homogeneous is inherently unstable, since the different effects of persistent force upon its various parts must cause differences to arise in their future development. Thus the homogeneous will inevitably develop into the heterogeneous. (Frost's version of this, in a poem of *In the Clearing*, is:

> A nation has to take its natural course
> Of Progress round and round in circles
> From King to Mob to King to Mob to King
> Until the eddy of it eddies out.

And this belief also throws light upon his presentation of the family unit, in many poems, as a pretty desolate structure.) And, finally, the Darwinian view is that all changes in types of survival and kinds of fitness are considered without relation to ultimate values; there is no relevant value beyond survival itself. There is, of course, a milder version of this to which we would all subscribe: "the desire of the body is to continue, the deepest need of the mind is for order," and where there is a quarrel, the body claims priority. But the Social Darwinists went much further than this.

If we look at a few of Frost's poems in this setting, the relation between his temperament and the ideas of Social Darwinism seems very close.

—Denis Donoghue, "Robert Frost," *Connoiseurs of Chaos: Ideas of Order in Modern American Poetry* (New York: Macmillan, 1965), pp. 181–83

⊛

FRANK LENTRICCHIA ON "MENDING WALL" IN RELATION TO OTHER POEMS IN *NORTH OF BOSTON*

[Frank Lentricchia is a professor of English and literature at Duke University and an important critic in American New Historicism. His works include *After the New Criticism* (1980) and *Criticism and Social Change* (1983). In this excerpt from *Robert Frost: Modern Poetics and the Landscapes of Self* (1975), Lentricchia describes how "Mending Wall" establishes the theme of maintaining "balance" that we see in later poems in the volume.]

"Mending Wall" is the opening poem of Frost's second volume, *North of Boston*. One of the dominating moods of this volume, forcefully established in such important poems as "The Death of the Hired Man," "Home Burial," "The Black Cottage," and "A Servant to Servants," and carried through some of the minor pieces, flows from the tension of having to maintain balance at the precipitous edge of hysteria. With "The Mountain" and with "A Hundred Collars," "Mending Wall" stands opposed to such visions of human existence; more precisely put, to existences that are fashioned by the neurotic visions of central characters like the wife in "Home Burial," the servant in "A Servant to Servants," "Mending Wall" dramatizes the redemptive imagination in its playful phase, guided surely and confidently by a man who has his world under full control, who in his serenity is riding his realities, not being shocked by them into traumatic response. The place of "Mending Wall" in the structure of *North of Boston* suggests, in its sharp contrasts to the dark tones of some of the major poems in the volume, the psychological necessities of sustaining supreme fictions.

The opening lines evoke the coy posture of the shrewd imaginative man who understands the words of the farmer in "The Mountain": "All the fun's in how you say a thing." [. . .] It does not take more than one reading of the poem to understand that the speaker is not a country primitive who is easily spooked by the normal processes of nature. He knows very well what it is "that doesn't love a wall" (Frost, of course). His fun lies in not naming it. And in not naming the scientific truth he is able to manipulate intransigent fact into the world of the mind where all things are pliable. The artful vagueness of the phrase "Something there is" is enchanting and magical, suggesting even the hushed tones of reverence before mystery in nature. And the speaker (who is not at all reverent toward nature) consciously works at deepening that sense of mystery. [. . .] The play of the mature, imaginative man is grounded in ironic awareness— and must be. Even as he excludes verifiable realities from his fictive world the unmistakable tone of scorn for the hunters comes seeping through. He may step into a fictive world but not before glancing back briefly at the brutality that attends upon the play of others. Having paid for his imaginative excursions by establishing his complex awareness, he is free to close the magic circle cast out by his playful energies, and close out the world reported by the senses ("No one has seen them made or heard them made"). In knowing how to say a thing in and through adroit linguistic manipulation, the fiction of the "something" that doesn't love a wall is created; the imagined reality stands formed before him, ready to be entered.

—Frank Lentricchia, *Robert Frost: Modern Poetics and the Landscapes of the Self* (Durham, N.C.: Duke University Press, 1975), pp. 103–05

⊛

Richard Poirier on Home in "The Death of the Hired Man"

[Richard Poirier is often considered Frost's foremost critic. A professor of English at Rutgers University and editor of the literary magazine *Raritan*, Poirier has published several books on American literature, including *The Performing Self* (1971), *Poetry and Pragmatism* (1992), and *Robert Frost: The Work of Knowing* (1977), from which this extract is taken. Poirier addresses Frost's portrayal of the dynamics of Mary and Warren's marital relationship.]

Frost was of many minds about "fences," "homes," or "yards." His genius as a narrative poet is in part his capacity to sustain debates between people about the nature of the "homes" which they very often occupy together. But it is a dangerous subject for him. It can encourage his tendency to wax idyllic about the possibilities of marital relationships, and this, in turn, sometimes reduces those possibilities for dramatic confrontation and for tension in dialogue that help make "Mending Wall" not only a humanly interesting but an intellectually rigorous poem. A dramatic narrative wherein differences of interpretation about "home" are more tenderly evoked is, of course, the poem which follows "Mending Wall" in *North of Boston*, "The Death of the Hired Man." It is significant that the poem was written in 1905–1906, a period when Frost was often romantically persuaded that "home" and "marriage" were the antidotes to poetic as well as personal sterility. Crucial to the poem is the discussion between the young husband and wife about whether or not a truant old field hand should be allowed to stay in their house now that he has decided to return, sick and probably unable to ever work again. [. . .]

The ambitious lunar sweep of the first two lines of this quotation [Part of a moon was falling down the west,/Dragging the whole sky with it to the hills] is brought into a human and domestic focus in the third line, when the light of the moon "poured softly in her lap." "She saw it,"—the sharpness of that clause, the more emphatic for its adding an extra accented syllable to the line, suggests that the wife is alert to the support she is getting from remote influences. It is a support she needs in her efforts to induce a benign mood in her husband toward the old man. Her gestures embrace these influences while they simultaneously reach out to play upon domestic artifacts—or may we call them props?—which are of her own making: the "morning-glory strings" that stretch from the "garden bed" to the eaves under which, most likely, is their marital "bed."

The tenderness that "wrought on him beside her in the night" can therefore be said to emanate not from her alone but from an environment, both natural and of her own creation. And it is this shared environment which is "their home." Since the issue of what to do about a difficult old man is in every way made subordinate to what is essentially a marriage idyll, there is no doubt about how the poetry wants the issue to be solved. There is a Miltonic tinge here, both in the scene and in the wife's way of arguing with her husband. She is assisted by the tender seductiveness of the world around them and assured of success by her prior knowledge of the inward disposition which has already put him there, "beside her in the night."

I am describing rather than promoting this kind of poem. Like "Directive," whose undoubted felicities of expression have already been sufficiently commended by Randall Jarrell, it belongs to Frost's elevated mode. And when Frost decides to be elevated he very often betrays to mere social commendability the more strenuous, aristocratic, courageous, visionary possibilities called into being by poems like "After Apple Picking" or "The Most of It." His tone is of one anxious to please those who want their elevation in an easy chair, and it is no accident that a remark as sentimonious as the wife's—that home is "something you somehow haven't to deserve"—should have become proverbial. Frost is close to selling out to his popular audience when he, or his characters, speak as if the environment around them adequately sustains their aspirations to hygienically fine feelings.

—Richard Poirier, *Robert Frost: The Work of Knowing* (New York: Oxford University Press, 1977), pp. 106–8 ℗

Katherine Kearns on Gender and Empathy in "The Death of the Hired Man"

[Katherine Kearns teaches at New York University and Yale University and is the author of *Robert Frost and a Poetics of Appetite* (1994), *Nineteenth-century Literary Realism* (1996), and *Psychoanalysis, Historiography, and Feminist Theory* (1997). Her critical perspective unites biography, psychology, deconstruction, and feminist analysis to elucidate Frost's poetics.]

In both "Home Burial" and "The Death of the Hired Man," the maternal solicitude that would hold and protect is enacted against the wishes of the adult male figure, who is ready to evict the "son" and move on to other things. Despite Mary's injunction to "Be kind," Warren calls Silas to account for his irresponsibility as regards work. He sees Silas as having chosen a relatively dissolute life, for if Silas has, admirably, rejected the corrupt values implicit in his brother's bank-director status, he has not consistently embraced any more reputable means by which a man may create order. Warren's concerns are economical and his attitude is juridical, and it is only when he is brought to remember that Silas could impose a small but perfect order in building a load of (usable, marketable) hay that he begins to be deterred from anger. He thinks legalistically, in terms of imperatives whose violation would result in some punishment: "Home is the place where, when you go there,/They have to take you in." Mary, whose heart "hurts" for Silas, sees home oppositely as "something you somehow haven't to deserve."

Such yielding as Mary would awaken in her husband is nonetheless a form of unmanning, almost a kind of bewitchment, as if she would bring Warren to be as ineffectual in worldly terms as the "son" Silas whose case she pleads. She is so tied to nature as that she is felt to play "the harp-like morning-glory strings, . . ./As if she played unheard some tenderness/That wrought on him beside her in the night," and she is felt to hold moonlight in her apron as naturally as a woman might sit with a lap full of apples to peel (or as naturally as the mountain of "The Birthplace" sits, "her lap . . . full of trees"). In Frost's landscape of named witches, Coös and Grafton the most notable, she seems to embody a relatively benign form of power, and she occupies a territory neither so pathologically scaled as the Witch of Coös nor so wild as the Witch of Grafton. Her position on the porch suggests a contained, somewhat domesticated form of power, yet she is so much a part of the earth and the night that she brings her husband out the door and shuts it, taking from his arms and setting aside the tokens of socialized domesticity, the "market things" with which he is so concerned. Mysterious, knowing, she is not merely a watcher but one of the elements—"Then there were three there, making a dim row,/The moon, the little silver cloud, and she"—and it is as if she *knows* and is thus potentially implicated in the spell by which the collision of moon with cloud will signal (cause) Silas's death. "The Death of the Hired Man" represents one of the most sustained visions of an apparently noncombative male-female relationship to be found anywhere in Frost's work, and yet implicit in Mary's great power to move Warren toward empathy is an equivalent power to remove him from control. Paradoxically, this poem reveals by its unusual status as a representative of marital harmony the dangers even a "good," domesticated female represents, as she threatens to co-opt rational judgment with emotion.

—Katherine Kearns, *Robert Frost and a Poetics of Appetite* (New York: Cambridge University Press, 1994), pp. 18–19

Thematic Analysis of
"The Oven Bird" and "Birches"
(including a discussion of "The Road Not Taken")

These three poems from *Mountain Interval* (1916), Frost's third book, offer perspectives on one of Frost's characteristic stances, a solitary figure in "mid-wood." As the title "Mountain Interval" suggests, these poems represent pauses in rural landscapes to contemplate the isolation, sometimes joyous and sometimes terrifying, that occurs "between"—between settlements, activities, and memories, as well as between the self and the natural world.

An oven bird is a plump, russet-crowned warbler that is typically found in mature North American forests. It is usually seen on the ground and builds domed, oven-shaped nests, from which it gets its name. Frost probably does not expect, as the first line claims, that "everyone has heard" an oven bird, nor to know that its distinctive call sounds like "teacher, teacher." By withholding this background information, Frost underscores a sense that the speaker has special knowledge of the environment presented.

Frost playfully ascribes a human intellect to the oven bird—an ability to "teach," to tell us "the way things are." This imputation of a communicative capacity to an animal occurs with slightly ironic coyness: the oven bird's "message," what the poem professes that "he says," clearly does not come from a bird. The bird represents the poet's own lyric voice, projected or "ventriloquized."

The bird gives instruction about the unstoppable seasonal progression from bloom to decay. By the time of midsummer's flourishing green, leaves are already old. With the mathematical precision and cool impersonality of a ratio, the bird "says" that for flowers, midsummer is as distant from spring as one is from 10; that is, their "days are numbered," and in the countdown of their brief life span, they are approaching the "one" that marks their demise.

This comment on the transience of bloom, the reminder that "early petal-fall is past" almost as soon as it has begun, signals the arrival of "that other fall." Brief moments of "overcast" foreshadow the oncoming autumn—ripeness and harvest lead ultimately to the death and decay of winter. The word "fall" is repeated three times in a span of four lines, and echoed in the definitive rhyme, "all." "Fall" is inescapable, suggesting also humanity's Fall, the Fall from grace, marked in the Western tradition by the biblical account of Adam's and Eve's eating of the forbidden fruit.

This bird would cease singing and be as other birds except that, paradoxically, he "knows in singing not to sing." He stands as a figure for the poet, but one who is only able to communicate in "all but words." In this tension between singing and saying, Frost comments on his own medium, language itself, noting that words only recall and approach their subjects, not invoke them. The language of a poem can memorialize material things but cannot command their presence or alter their "diminishment," their inevitable "fall." How the poet contends with this state of affairs, as well as other "diminished things," including frustrated hopes and his own aging, becomes the central concern of the poem.

The last thing the bird "says," that "the highway dust is over all," implies the return to dust of all living creatures, in particular humans who toil in their "travelling"—literally, through a wood, and figuratively, through a life. Frost's "mid-wood" scene alludes obliquely to Dante, whose journey in *The Divine Comedy* begins in a dark wood "in the middle of life's way." Frost published *Mountain Interval* at the age of 42, and "The Oven Bird" explores this "middle of the journey" state of mind, especially "what to make of" poetry and his own poetic gift at this juncture.

It is no accident that this meditation on the power of "song" and poetry is scrupulously constructed as a sonnet. At the traditional "turn" in the poem's argument in the ninth line, "And comes that other fall. . . ," Frost shifts from the oven bird's announcement of the impermanence of the lush summer world to the contemplation of the limited capacity to "sing" about it. "The Oven Bird" has two quatrains rhyming *aabc* and *bdcd*, followed by a sestet that rhymes *eefgfg*, a slight loosening of the sonnet's rhyming strictures to accommodate the conversational tone. Frost's skillful variations on the iambic pentameter underscore the poem's message with musical effects. The second line begins with a stressed syllable that emphasizes the "loud" quality of the bird's song, for example, and the strong stresses of "tree trunks sound" convey their solidity (line three). The breezy iambic lines that rush us through the progress of the "petal-fall" mimic the effect of rapid descent they describe.

"Birches," by contrast, presents a different look at "diminished things." The poem begins with the clear understanding that the trees the speaker sees have been bent down by ice storms, not by a boy swinging on them, as the speaker would prefer to believe. Frost describes the storm in images of chilling beauty that suggest an immense power in the weather capable of bringing down "the inner dome of heaven." In this image, the poem announces its conscious relation to a literary tradition, alluding to Percy Bysshe Shelley's line "Life, like a dome of many-colored glass" in Adonais, and John Milton's cosmogony of the "starry sphere" of the universe in *Paradise Lost*. When Frost rewrites the "cause" of the arching trees, he also partly rewrites a long-standing literary trope for human vision of the cosmos—he brings the sky "earthward."

By using a casual idiom and a forthright second person address ("you must have seen them") to engage the question of causality in nature, Frost gives the poem a conversational immediacy, as if he were talking to a neighbor. When the speaker interrupts the description of the ice storm ("But I was going to say when Truth broke in"), he then turns to a more fanciful interpretation of the cause of the bent trees: in contrast with the clear-sighted, factual explanation of nature's destructive violence, he imagines "some boy's been swinging them."

The scene that follows operates partly within the conventions of pastoral poetry in its suggestion of an idyllic, rustic life of solitude, but it also alters those conventions. This country youth resembles the shepherd of the pastoral, as he is sent "to fetch the cows." Yet, he chooses to entertain himself with a different kind of artistry than song. He practices a carefully choreographed effort to "subdue his father's trees/By riding them down over and over again." The imagery of this landscape reveals a sexual subtext, as subdued phallic trees suggest Frost's ambivalence about asserting masculine power in the face of nature. Here, nature is not always simple and serene, as the pastoral would have it. The boy's "dream" of "conquering" is deliberately invoked to counter the harsh reality of an inhospitable world where vulnerability and pain—as in the image of the eye lashed by the twig—are all too common.

Frost's central figure in this poem is a "swinger of birches," but the speaker is a "*singer* of birches" who transforms, through poetry, a comparison between natural and human causes into a metaphor for how to live. The scene of the boy's playing is so vivid that we begin to take it for the truer explanation, forgetting the earlier disclaimer, and this shift is part of Frost's point: The more whimsical evocations of memory have a greater psychological weight than factual accounts. Facilitating this point, Frost makes sure we feel and hear the verse as much as we envision the scene. In the line "Kicking his way down through the air to the ground," Frost varies the iambic line with anapests to evoke the quick and light motion of the boy's surrender to gravity. In the remarkable image of the cup over-brimming, we sense the palpable tension of the boy's limber poise and assurance.

Reading this familiar poem, which Frost often read publicly, one is tempted to think of Frost's poetry in terms of his reputation as a cheerful, grandfatherly, homespun poet. Many readers and critics have challenged this view as overlooking Frost's far more complex stance toward nature and its darker forces. Literary critic Lionel Trilling (1905–1975) famously assessed Frost's work as presenting a "terrifying universe." Either view—one that assumes "country" optimism or one that sees only emptiness, violence, or despair—is oversimplified.

"Birches" is indeed nostalgic, but it also explores the underpinnings of the temptation to both of these responses. Climbing birch trees becomes an extended metaphor for the speaker's wish to approach heaven and yet be returned to the human world we know—a world that is neither always idyllic nor always horrifying. By claiming "Earth's the right place for love," Frost replaces a vision of a redemptive afterlife with a wish to remain in the material universe with all of its complications and threats of "diminishment." The poem likewise calls into question our complicity in the "willful misunderstanding" of the speaker's revision of the scene through memory. We can indulge a fantasy of perfect control of nature but must also accept the darker forces that indeed compromise our fate.

Both "The Oven Bird" and "Birches" address themes we find in Frost's oft-quoted "The Road Not Taken," the poem that begins *Mountain Interval.* It, too, takes up the matter of a critical juncture "midway." Contrary to a common misreading, the two roads that diverge in a yellow wood do not show any marked difference: "the passing there/had worn them really about the same." The notion that one road is less traveled than the other is a *fiction,* a story the speaker "shall be telling" "ages and ages hence." The poem emphasizes the arbitrary nature of our choices, choices which later take on the character of a fated significance once they have crystallized in memory. What makes "all the difference" is the speaker's self-fiction of forging his own "less traveled" path. This poem is as difficult as it is popular. (Frost himself insisted it was a tricky poem.) As in "The Oven Bird," where "highway dust is over all," the uniform landscape in this poem obscures the possibility of human motivation and choice. As in "Birches," where "life is too much like a pathless wood," it addresses the weariness of "considerations." Nonetheless, it identifies the poignancy of any mid-wood meeting of self with world: "way leads on to way," and, as the title emphasizes, "The Road *Not* Taken"—not the one that *was*—tends to become the subject of reflection. ❀

Critical Views on
"The Oven Bird" and "Birches"

PETER VIERECK COMPARES FROST TO OTHER MODERNIST POETS

[Peter Viereck is a poet, critic, and historian. He is also the author of *Dream and Responsibility: Four Test Cases of the Tension between Poetry and Society* (1953) and *Conservatism: From John Adams to Churchill* (1956). In this contemporary review of *Frost's Complete Poems*, which he calls "the most important book of 1949," Viereck argues that Frost has been overlooked by "higher criticism" because of misunderstood differences between his work and that of the avant-garde.]

Robert Frost's name is rarely heard among the exquisites of *avant-garde*. His poems are like those plants that flourish in the earth of the broad plains and valleys but will not strike root in more rarefied atmospheres. The fact remains that he is one of the world's greatest living poets. Frost, W. H. Auden, Wallace Stevens, and William Carlos Williams are the contemporary poets in America whose styles are most intensely original, most unmistakably their own. Of the four, Frost is the only one to be widely read in terms of general circulation and the only one who has never been adequately subjected to the Higher Criticism of the *doctores subtiles* of the Little Magazines.

On first reading, Frost seems easier than he really is. This helps account for both the enormous number of his readers, some of whom like him for wrong or irrelevant reasons, and for the indifference of the coteries, who become almost resentful when they can find no double-crostics to solve. Frost's cheerfulness is often mistaken as smug, folksy, Rotarian. This fact, plus his reputation for a solid New England conservatism, frightens away rebel youth and "advanced" professors.

In truth, his cheerfulness is the direct opposite of Mr. Babbitt's or even of Mr. Pickwick's. It is a Greek cheerfulness. And the apparent blandness of the Greeks was, as Nietzsche showed in his *Birth of Tragedy*, the result of their having looked so deeply into life's tragic meaning that they had to protect themselves by cultivating a deliberately superficial jolliness in order to bear the unbearable. Frost's benign calm, the comic mask of a whittling rustic, is designed for gazing—without dizziness—into a tragic abyss of desperation. This is the same eternal abyss that gaped not only for the Hellenes but for such moderns as Pascal, Kierkegaard, Nietzsche, Baudelaire, Kafka. "Pascal," wrote Baudelaire, "had his abyss that followed him." In the case of this great New England tragic poet, the desperation is no less real for being a quiet one, as befits a master of overwhelming under-statements. His almost too smooth quietness is a booby trap to spring [. . .] ruthless doubt. [. . .]

A word about his metrics and his diction. Frost is one of the few poets today who dare use contractions like "as 'twere" and "e'er." I don't care for this sort of thing, especially in a poet who makes a point of catching the idiom of everyday speech. But I don't let this annoying anachronism spoil my enjoyment of him. Equally old-fashioned, but this time in a better sense of the word, is the fact that his meters scan with a beat-by-beat regularity, usually in the form of rhymed iambic pentameters. In this connection, do not overlook his thoughtful preface on poetic techniques and meters.

Frost's stubborn conventionality of form makes many young poets and readers think his is also a conventionality of meaning. On the contrary, he is one of the most original writers of our time. It is the self-conscious *avant-garde* rebels who follow the really rigid and tiresome conventions.

—Peter Viereck, "Parnassus Divided," *Atlantic Monthly* 184 (October 1949): 67–8

YVOR WINTERS ON FROST AS A ROMANTIC POET

[Yvor Winters (1900–1968), American poet, critic, and longtime professor at Stanford University, was a key figure among the New Critics. His critical works include *Primitivism and Decadence* (1937), *The Anatomy of Nonsense* (1943), and *The Function of Criticism* (1957), from which this extract is taken. Winters is highly critical of Frost, describing the limitations of his use of rural settings and his conversational style, and considering his relation to Emerson and the American Romantic tradition.]

Frost writes of rural subjects, and the American reader of our time has an affection for rural subjects which is partly the product of the Romantic sentimentalization of "nature," but which is partly also a nostalgic look back to the rural life which predominated in this nation a generation or two ago; the rural life is somehow regarded as the truly American life. I have no objection to the poet's employing rural settings; but we should remember that it is the poet's business to evaluate human experience, and the rural setting is no more valuable for this purpose than any other or than no particular setting, and one could argue with some plausibility that an exclusive concentration on it may be limiting.

Frost early began his endeavor to make his style approximate as closely as possible the style of conversation, and this endeavor has added to his reputation: it has helped to make him seem "natural." But poetry is not conversation, and I see no reason why poetry should be called upon to imitate conversation. Conversation is the most careless and formless of human utterance; it is spontaneous and unrevised, and its vocabulary is commonly limited. Poetry is the most difficult form of human utterance; we revise poems carefully in order to make them more nearly perfect. The two forms of expression are extremes, they are not close to each other. We do not praise a violinist for playing as if he were improvising; we praise him for playing well. And when a man plays well or writes well, his audience must have intelligence, training, and patience in order to appreciate him. We do not understand difficult matters "naturally." [...]

Frost has said that Emerson is his favorite American poet, and he himself appears to be something of an Emersonian. Emerson was a Romantic pantheist: he identified God with the universe; he taught that impulse comes directly from God and should be obeyed, that through surrender to impulse we become one with God; he taught that reason is man-made and bungling and should be suppressed. In moral and aesthetic doctrine, his most thorough-going disciples in American literature were Walt Whitman and Hart Crane. In Frost, on the other hand, we find a disciple without Emerson's religious conviction: Frost believes in the rightness of impulse, but does not discuss the pantheistic doctrine which would give authority to

impulse; as a result of his belief in impulse, he is of necessity a rela-
tivist, but his relativism, apparently since it derives from no intense
religious conviction, has resulted mainly in ill-natured eccentricity
and in increasing melancholy. He is an Emersonian who has become
sceptical and uncertain without having reformed; and the scepticism
and uncertainty do not appear to have been so much the result of
thought as the result of the impact upon his sensibility of conflicting
notions of his own era—they appear to be the result of his having
taken the easy way and having drifted with the various currents of
his time.

—Yvor Winters, "Robert Frost: Or, The Spiritual Drifter as Poet," *The
Function of Criticism* (Denver: Alan Swallow, 1957), pp. 160, 162

⊗

John F. Lynen on Pastoralism and Frost as a Nature Poet

[John Lynen was a professor of English at the University of
Toronto and is the author of *The Design of the Present: Essays
on Time and Form in American Literature* (1969) and *The Pastoral Art of Robert Frost* (1960), from which this extract is
taken. Lynen explores how Frost's poems operate within
some of the conventions of the pastoral genre but also present nature as essentially distant from human beings.]

Frost has so often written about the rural landscape and wildlife that
one can hardly avoid thinking of him as a nature poet. "To the
Thawing Wind," "Hyla Brook," "The Oven Bird," "Birches," "A
Drumlin Woodchuck"—one could cite such titles by the score. Frost
began as a nature poet; "To a Moth Seen in Winter," "Rose Pogonias,"
"Going for Water" are representative of his work before 1913, and
the interest in nature was to persist throughout his career. Frost's
nature poetry is so excellent and so characteristic that it must be
given a prominent place in any account of his art. In our attempt to
understand this aspect of Frost, the idea of the pastoral proves
useful. Not that the nature poems are to be considered as pastorals
in any strict sense—obviously the two kinds of poetry differ. In pastorals the subject is a special society, or, more generally, a way of life,

and nature is merely the setting within which we see this. The pastoralist does not write *about* nature; he uses nature as his scene, and it is important only in that it defines the swain's point of view. Nevertheless, Frost's nature poetry is closely related to his pastoralism. One might demonstrate the connection by pointing out how many poems combine both genres. Such pieces as "The Onset," "Unharvested," and "Evening in a Sugar Orchard" present vivid pictures of landscape, but in them the Yankee point of view through which nature is seen is as vital to the meaning as the things portrayed. This is not so in all the nature poems: in a great many others natural objects hold the center of interest, and the regional Arcadia with its Yankee characters is absent or unimportant. The shift in subject is not surprising, for a poet of rural life would find it natural to write about the countryside, but the connection between the two poetic types is more fundamental than this. It consists, I think, in a similarity of thought, and hence, in a similarity of poetic design. The basic structure we have noted in his eclogues appears again as the dominant pattern in the nature poems. Both kinds of poetry seem to grow from a singular way of looking at reality—the same perspective which creates pastorals when the poet's eyes are directed to rural life determines his vision of nature. [. . .]

In both his nature poems and his pastorals the poet portrays average human experience by projecting it into a world remote and distinct. Nature, as Frost conceives it, is really a kind of wild-life Arcadia, and in writing of scenery and animals he uses it in much the same way as he uses the mythical rural New England in his pastorals. Like his rural New England, nature evokes paradoxical attitudes: on the one hand it is a realm of ideals where the essential realities are found in their pristine forms; on the other it is an inferior plane where life is crude, insensate, mechanical. Most important, however, nature is separate, independent, off by itself away from man, just as the country north of Boston is separate from the urban environment of modern America.

—John F. Lynen, *The Pastoral Art of Robert Frost* (New Haven: Yale University Press, 1960), pp. 140–1, 153

[Robert Pack, a professor of literature at Middlebury College, is a poet and the director of Breadloaf Writer's Conference. His books include several collections of poetry and *Affirming Limits: Essays on Mortality, Choice, and Poetic Form* (1985). In this extract, he considers the poet's role as a "maker of belief."]

The season of fall is linked in "The Oven Bird" with the fall from the garden of Eden by the poetic act of naming: "And comes that other fall we name the fall." The poet has merged his voice with the oven bird, as Adam, in the book of Genesis, names the animals. So, too, the linking of literal meanings, speech, with poetic meanings, song, accomplishes the design by which the total poem exists in its own form and its own right. It is both sung prose and spoken song that enables Frost—as an oven bird—to know "in singing not to sing," for as speech can become song, and song can incorporate speech (as it does in this poem), so, too, can fact become metaphor, and metaphor, fact. These are the linkings that constitute poetic truth.

Belief for Frost is always grounded in the questions out of which belief emerges. As the maker of belief, this is what Frost teaches and what the poet proclaims is the virtual effect of the bird's song, which in reality is Frost's poem: "The question that he [both Frost and the oven bird] frames in all but words." The question is framed, just as the form of the sonnet constitutes a structural frame, and thus the question *implies* more than the words themselves can literally ask. The question embodies the *feeling* of the enigma of what man can make of himself and of his world: "Remember that the sentence sound often says more than the words," Frost once asserted. It is only because (like the bird's song) the poem is framed, because it is a made thing, that the question it asks, and the answer of belief that it implies, can remain dynamically in tension. The poem remains open to the reader's own scrutiny. Such is the style of Frostian teaching.

The question asked by the oven bird is "what to make of a diminished thing." It comes at the end of the poem and thus it throws us back to the beginning, so that the poem makes a kind of circle. But the question, though specific enough, is also enigmatic: What "diminished thing"? Summer is a diminishing from spring, as the oven bird says, "as one to ten." Fall is a diminishing from summer.

The fall from the garden of Eden is a mythical diminishing. Death, the highway "dust," is the diminishment of life. (What can one make of death?) The poem is a diminishing of the oven bird's loud call and its *possible* meanings. (All poetic form is made by choice and selection and is thus a diminishing of nature's plenitude.) Aging on the highway, Frost, too, is a diminishing thing. The poem itself, however, is the poet's only answer to these questions, for it is, indeed, what the poet has made. It is an order, a design, to set against uncertainty, to set against "the fall" and against death. As Frost consoled, "When in doubt there is always form for us to go on with." And thus the reader is left with the enigma of what to make of the poem, a thing "diminished" into shape from the chaos of life. Frost offers us a man-made form, and it is for us to be strengthened by it as such, to find in its own framed coherence what Frost himself believed to be there, "a momentary stay against confusion." And those readers who actually have heard the call of an oven bird (or have looked it up in Roger Tory Peterson's *A Field Guide to the Birds*) will know that what the oven bird says is: "Teacher! Teacher!"

—Robert Pack, "Frost's Enigmatical Reserve: The Poet as Teacher and Preacher," *Affirming Limits: Essays on Mortality, Choice, and Poetic Form* (Amherst: University of Massachusetts Press, 1985), pp. 177–8

JAMES ELLIS ON REPRESENTATIONS OF SEXUAL GROWTH IN "BIRCHES"

[James Ellis is a professor of English at the University of North Carolina at Greensboro and has published several articles on American literature. In this extract, Ellis examines how stages of erotic, procreative, and artistic belief underlie the poem.]

"Birches" (*Poetry* 121–22) is a poem divided into two parts. The first part celebrates the boy's sexual growth and the erotic, spiritual dream of climbing "Toward heaven" (122) that accompanies this growth. The boy's swinging of the birches in pursuit of this dream is a metaphor for masturbation and represents Frost's concept of "the self-belief."

The second part of the poem evolves from the boy's "self-belief" and describes the mature man who moves from the solitary, erotic dream of the boy to a relationship with another human being, a woman whom he loves and with whom he joins in "the love-belief." The "love-belief" of this man and woman is necessarily a relation of human being to human being, of matter relating to matter. For this reason, as the man says, "Earth's the right place for love" (122). The result of this "love-belief," the poem suggests, is the birth of children.

Finally both stages of belief—erotic "self-belief" and procreative "love-belief"—are mirrored in the poem to create the "art-belief" that serves to lead both poet and reader toward "the God-belief" and the effort of man "to bring about the future."

The poem begins with the mature man's commenting on the effect of ice storms upon the birch trees, how the ice storms bend them down to stay, and his preference instead that a boy might have been swinging them and for once had bent them down to stay. Frost then proceeds to describe the kind of boy who is a swinger of birches. He is solitary, a "boy too far from town to learn baseball,/Whose only pay was what he found himself . . . and could play alone" (121). "One by one," Frost writes, "he subdued his father's trees" (122). We assume on the basis of this line that, in turn, the boy's father—before *his* father's farm—he also had swung and subdued his father's birches in his own expression of "the self-belief."

The boy subdues the birches "[b]y riding them down over and over again/Until he took the stiffness out of them,/And not one but hung limp, not one was left/For him to conquer" (122). And this swinging of birches, this masturbatory play, is informed by a spiritual quest, for he climb[s] black branches up a snow-white trunk/*Toward* heaven" (122). The erect birches function then as a representation of the boy's phallic sexuality and his erotic impulse toward the spiritual—in Frost's words, "to say spirit in terms of matter" ("Education" 41).

But Frost does more with the image of the birches than leave them to serve only as a phallic representation. For the birches function in their delicate whiteness as an image not only of the erect male member, but also—in much the same manner as "The Silken Tent"—of the physical girl who represents the boy's heavenly aspiration and with whom he would imagine the act of sexual intercourse. For in describing the boy's climbing the white trunk, Frost plays upon the sexual meaning of the verb "to climb," which from the early seventeenth century has been used as a metaphor for "the mount[ing]" and having sexual intercourse with a woman (Spears 75).

Frost's representation of sexual growth and artistic play continues with his description of the boy's learning process as he becomes more and more expert in the art of climbing and swinging birches. [. . .]

These two beliefs then, "the self-belief" of the boy and "the love-belief" of the man, are united and find their expression in the poem, which in turn is Frost's rendering of the third of his beliefs, "the art-belief." And these forms of belief are, for Frost, our "momentary stay[s] against confusion" ("Figure" 18) and the means whereby we may come to "the God-belief" and thereby enter into "a relationship . . . with Him [in order] to bring about the future" ("Education" 45).

—James Ellis, "Robert Frost's Four Types of Belief in 'Birches,'" *The Robert Frost Review* (1993): 71-3

⟨֍⟩

MATTHEW PARFITT ON FROST'S MODERN GEORGICS

[Matthew Parfitt is an assistant professor of humanities at Boston University. In this extract, Parfitt argues that Frost's poems are best understood not in the pastoral tradition but as georgics, which address the realities of farming.]

The severity of much of Frost's poetry confounds the expectations raised by pastoral, and the assumption that Frost belongs to this tradition predisposes the reader to overlook the importance of georgic themes—centering on work and the earth—in Frost's vision. Indeed, it may be that the widespread opinion that Frost is an exceptionally "dark" poet derives from the sense that he has played a malicious trick on the unsuspecting reader by failing to depict Arcadia. But Frost's vision of nature is not so much bleak as unflinching; and this attitude is consistent with the georgic perspective, in which nature is not an idealized stage-set but the context of a struggle for subsistence, a struggle at least to stand still "in the rush of everything to waste" ("The Master Speed" *CP* 392). "Build Soil" from *A Further Range* is a telling example: in form, it is a thoroughly pastoral philosophical dialogue between characters named Tityrus and Meliboeus—but the burden is unmistakably georgic: "Build soil. Turn the farm in upon itself/Until it can contain itself no more,/But sweating-full, drips wine and oil a little" (*CP* 428).

In the Middle Ages, the *rota Virgilii* (Virgil's wheel)—the cycle of pastoral, georgic, and epic represented by Virgil's works—stood not only for the stages of a poet's career as he advanced through a hierarchy of styles—*stilus humilis, stilus mediocris, stilus gravis*—but for a hierarchy in the nature of things, among human activities (playing, working, fighting), social ranks (shepherd, farmer, soldier), tools (crook, plow, sword), locales (pasture, field, castle/city), and so on (Curtius 201n, 231-2; Low 4). According to this tradition, pastoral and georgic are quite distinct genres. Pastoral is fundamentally escapist and artificial; even when, as in Virgil's *Eclogues*, the concerns are philosophical and political rather than erotic, they are hardly those of real shepherds. Corydon and Tityrus are courtiers in fancy dress, who speak in urbane, literary voices; and Arcadia is a device by which to draw the contrast between the innocent pleasures of the shepherd's leisure and the distracted, decadent luxury of the city and the court. The four books of the *Georgics*, on the other hand, celebrate not *otium* (leisure) but *labor*, the work of the farmer and the abundance of the responsive earth. [...]

Both Virgil and Frost are acutely conscious of a "fall;" but if one considers Frost's poetry in its relation to georgic, this appears less as pessimistic irony than as a sense of the richness of what remains. Just as Virgil shows that the labor of the farmer is "organically related to the processes of nature, dignified and also beautiful in its own right" (Griffin 45), so Frost finds the dignity and poignancy of things to be the greater for being somehow diminished, for being less than perfect. "We love the things we love for what they are" he decides in "Hyla Brook"; and in "Mowing," "The fact is the sweetest dream that labor knows." The georgic theme itself entails an ethical purpose: Virgil and Frost both feel it man's destiny to row upstream against the current (*Georgics* I, 199ff)— "It is this backward motion toward the source,/Against the stream, that most we see ourselves in,/The tribute of the current to the source" (CP 329)—and this produces a poetry in which exhortation and moral dictum have their place. Frost may sometimes overindulge in these; but as the issue of georgic reflections, his gnomic sentences are not the imposition they might be elsewhere. Philosophical insight in Frost's poetry after *A Boy's Will* arises not from the speaker's musing at leisure, as in pastoral, but from a conjunction of human labor and the "facts," the things themselves in their brute difference from consciousness and indifference to desire. This may be another reason for Frost's popularity: it is the poetry of work, and this speaks both to the desire to recover a lost contact with *things* and to work as the almost universal fact of modern life. Frost's New England is not Arcadia, not a tame place apart, but a place that is familiar without being prosaic.

—Matthew Parfitt, "Robert Frost's 'Modern Georgics,'" *The Robert Frost Review* (1996): 54–55, 67

H. A. MAXSON ON THE OVEN BIRD AS A FIGURE FOR THE POET

[H. A. Maxson is the author of *On the Sonnets of Robert Frost* (1997). Maxson offers a reading of "The Oven Bird" that stresses Frost's identification with the bird as a figure for his poetic powers.]

In his biography of Frost, William Pritchard tells the story of Sidney Cox, a student of Frost's, perusing *Mountain Interval* then writing to Frost addressing him as "Dear Oven Bird," rather than "Mr. Frost." Cox believed that he had discovered a "key" to understanding Frost. However, Frost insisted that Cox made too much of the poem and dismissed his praise and his insight. But Pritchard suggests that Cox was indeed on to something, that perhaps this was one of the doors in the poems that Frost spoke of but one not secured fast enough, leaving the student the opportunity to view the master unguarded where it was left ajar.

And such an interpretation seems fair enough. "What he frames in all but words" is certainly tantalizingly close to "the sound of sense" theory Frost developed. On any number of levels, according to the biographies, Frost felt himself to be a "diminished thing." As Cox rightly pointed out, Frost's voice was not loud, but it had been heard—if not by "everyone" then at least by a significant number of important listeners. And Frost the popularizer was certainly at work making sure his poems and books were read—if not at the time the poems were written, then when they were published ten or more years later.

In that regard it is worth suggesting that this poem, written in the same period as the sonnets of *A Boy's Will*, perhaps takes up an image introduced in "Into My Own," that of the trees, metaphorically the solid poetic giants of the nineteenth century whom Frost admired and boasted/threatened/promised to move among in that poem. If that is the case, then the speaker in "The Oven Bird" has achieved that distinction, at least in his own mind, when he says, "Who makes the solid tree trunks sound again." [. . .]

What we have then are two distinct poems or two very different readings of one poem—two ways of saying one thing in terms of another. Ostensibly the sonnet is about a bird, a teacher bird (another name for it), and its song that is no song at all but a jumble of notes concluding with *teacher teacher*, which makes it distinct from other birds. The diminished thing is himself or the world immediately around him, the season, what have you.

A personal reading of the poem says it is about the poet, as Cox saw it, the singer who has craftily, modernistically, learned to avoid the obvious eccentricities and pomposities of the nineteenth century and to use the sound of everyday speech; hence he has learned "in singing not to sing." The poet views the world around him, his own arrival at middle age, the diminution of the beauty of youth that comes during the blink of an eye, "a moment overcast." He has, finally, achieved the escape that played so heavily in *A Boy's Will*, and in a sense has avoided some of the "highway dust" that coats the world—but not completely, for it "is over all." The diminished thing is himself, his own life. At about the time of the publication of *Mountain Interval* he confided in Louis Untermeyer, perhaps only half teasingly, that the poet in him had died ten years before. This was an exaggeration, to be sure, but it does give credence to the reading of the final line as being a reference to himself, as well as his own beliefs about himself and perhaps his poetic powers.

—H. A. Maxson, *On the Sonnets of Robert Frost* (Jefferson, N.C.: McFarland & Co., 1997), pp. 40–2 ☙

Thematic Analysis of
"Design"
(including a discussion of "Fire and Ice")

The speaker of this poem happens upon an outdoor scene that has three "players," "assorted characters of death and blight": a white flower called a "heal-all," a snow-drop spider, and a moth. The moth, attracted to the white of the flower, has been caught by the spider. "Death" and "blight" are strong terms that suggest a plague or curse, but Frost introduces them so glibly that at first we do not wince at this spectacle of predator and prey. A lighthearted tone eases us into what becomes a frightening look at the forces that compel these ultimately violent events to come to pass. The moth cannot help but be attracted to the white flower, where it alights only to be devoured. The spider cannot help but devour it. Through a microcosm that suggests larger significance, the poem presents a darkly pessimistic look at an unavoidable chain of events—unavoidable in a way especially unfortunate for the moth

The moth is immediately transformed, held up "like a white piece of rigid satin cloth." It becomes a piece of "formal material" in two senses—it is likened to an elegant fabric, and it becomes an art object displayed for contemplation. The spider's gesture of "holding up" invokes images of a ritual sacrifice, a kind of natural-world "black mass." The characters are ready "to begin the morning fight," and "right" suggests its homophone: they are assembled to begin the morning "rite." The mix of "ingredients of a witches' broth" is something at once delicious and wicked. By the poem's sixth line, we are fully aware the poem is addressing the presence of some kind of evil in the world, but we do not know whether we should be genuinely horrified by a satanic act of murder or entertained by its playful imitation. Should we relish the notion of witchcraft with its macabre-humorous "antics," as we would a Halloween skit, or should we condemn it? Is the poem a serious caution or a funny, diabolical rag? The poem invites us to notice both of these responses.

The poem is made even more startling because it considers evil forces in a guise of happy domesticity. The word "dimpled" is both homely and grotesque. As critic Mordecai Marcus has pointed out, the albino spider is described as if it were a baby—something that if it were called dimpled, fat, and white might also be called "cute." A spider with those same characteristics is shudderingly awful. The poem proceeds with simple diction that could have come from a children's story, and its quick-paced meter reminds one of a nursery rhyme. The poem also suggests the language of breakfast cereal advertisements, as critic Randall Jarrell has observed. When the "ingredients" of the "broth" are reiterated in line seven, the poem recommends starting the day off right—not with a good breakfast, but with a decidedly unwholesome scene of consumption.

Any seeming frivolity, however, is quickly undercut by the more menacing question of "design." Undertones of ominousness culminate in the question of what "brought" or "steered" the creatures to this bleak configuration. Several unrelated and chance occurrences lead to the "sacrifice": a heal-all is normally blue, but this one is white; a spider has climbed to the top of the flower; a moth has been lured by some instinct to end up in the spider's path. Is it a "design of darkness," the plan of some malevolent deity or evil force in the universe, that orchestrated these events in sequence? At the ninth line, the poem shifts into an interrogative mode, and the reader is led to assume an almost juridical frame of mind. Who or what is to blame for this scene of death? Is anyone? Can we attribute premeditation anywhere, or, even if we could, would there be any fault?

The poem raises these questions of agency and necessity in the natural world, but it does not offer a theodicy, an explanation of the origin of evil and the reason for it. Instead, Frost leaves us with an ambivalent sense that a conflict of good and evil, light and darkness, underlies all natural processes, and that evil seems to win out. The complex resonances of two words focus this tension. The spider is described as "kindred," but the very propinquity it has with other creatures makes it threatening, not protective. The design is said to "appall," to shock or horrify, and Frost plays on the word's derivation from "to grow or make pale, whiten." The color white dominates the poem's visual images (describing the spider, moth, flower), and the word "white" is used four times, dominating the poem's rhymes as well (exactly *half* of the lines end with a word that rhymes with "white"). With the word "appall," the predominance of white on white leads to the conclusion that "to whiten" is not to purify but to grow pallid, afflicted—to whiten to *death*, not to innocence.

"Design," moreover, is a highly *designed* poem, a Petrarchan sonnet. It has a tight interlocking rhyme scheme with two *abba* octaves, followed by a sestet that picks up the *a*-rhyme (-ite) again, *acaacc.* The relentless rhyming—through simple monosyllables that remain unobtrusive—furthers a sense of inescapable unity that the poem as a whole explores. The rhymes themselves set off striking associations—to rhyme "heal-all" and "appall" is to join two divergent alternatives—a panacea and a power to alarm—to force the reader to consider a relationship between them. This "heal-all" has no curative function, becoming instead an accessory to killing. With two rhyming couplets concluding the poem, the argument "clicks shut," a tidy wrap-up that also underscores a sense of inevitability

Frost's poem forces the reader to make a very uncomfortable choice: Either there is no design in nature, and the described sequence of events is completely accidental, or there is a design, and it's an evil one. Perhaps one of the most disturbing consequences of such a choice is its relation to *art* and how we encounter it. Through formal symmetries and exactitudes, the poem draws attention to its own making as a further example of "design." If evil governs "design" in the world, does it also govern the design of a sonnet?

The poem flourishes its aesthetic perfections, and Frost seems to delight in toying with the compositional power that makes the ordinary shocking. He employs four similes with a masterful and apt precision. The flower "like a froth" subtly implies the horror of something ravenous or rabid. This image starkly juxtaposes the image of the dead moth's wings compared to "a paper kite," a delicate toy. That *both* images can be suggested to the observer in quick succession makes the nature of poetic comparison seem disconcertingly arbitrary. At the mercy of the poet's comparisons, we are led to witness fluctuations from the perfectly beautiful to the just-as-perfectly awful.

A poem with similar concerns about world-governing oppositions, Frost's familiar "Fire and Ice" is memorable and highly quotable but deceptive in its surface simplicity. Like "Design," it makes use of chiming rhymes and fluctuating tones to construct an uneasy balance between two seemingly incompatible moods—a surety in its claims, and a noncommittal stance toward them, as if the speaker were shrugging his shoulders. On one hand, the poem's epigrammatic concision makes its musings on the potential for apocalypse sound certain, indisputable. On the other, phrases like "some say," "those who favor," and "I think" convey an amiable, conversational tentativeness. The resounding rhyme of "desire" and "fire" links the two terms forcibly, and we cannot help but agree that the heat of passion has its destructive side, the sound enforcing our agreement. Likewise, the coy and understated "suffice" rhymes with the "ice" of hatred to suggest another indisputable equation for the apocalypse. Frost's binaries, framed as offhand quips and edged with irony, allow their terms to imply each other and force us to examine the artificiality of their construction. ❀

Critical Views on
"Design"

RANDALL JARRELL ON FROST'S DARKER SIDE

[Randall Jarrell (1914–1965), American poet, novelist, and critic, revitalized the reputations of Frost, Walt Whitman (1819–1892), and William Carlos Williams (1883–1963) in the 1950s. His works of criticism include *Poetry and the Age* (1953), *A Sad Heart at the Supermarket* (1962), and *The Third Book of Criticism* (1969). In this extract, Jarrell challenges the popular view of Frost as an accessible and optimistic poet, offering "Design" as exemplifying "the other Frost."]

Besides the Frost that everybody knows there is one whom no one even talks about. Everybody knows what the regular Frost is: the one living poet who has written *good* poems that ordinary readers like without any trouble and understand without any trouble; the conservative editorialist and self-made apothegm-joiner, full of dry wisdom and free, complacent, Yankee enterprise; the Farmer-Poet— this is an imposing private rôle perfected for public use, a sort of Olympian Will Rogers out of *Tanglewood Tales;* and, last or first of all, Frost is the standing, speaking reproach to any other good modern poet: "If Frost can write poetry that's just as easy as Longfellow you can too—you do too." It is this "easy" side of Frost that is most attractive to academic readers, who are eager to canonize any modern poet who condemns in example the modern poetry which they condemn in precept; and it is this side that has helped to get him neglected or depreciated by intellectuals—the reader of Eliot or Auden usually dismisses Frost as something inconsequentially good that *he* knew all about long ago. Ordinary readers think Frost the greatest poet alive, and love some of his best poems almost as much as they love some of his worst ones. He seems to them a sensible, tender, humorous poet who knows all about trees and farms and folks in New England, and still has managed to get an individualistic, fairly optimistic, thoroughly American philosophy out of what he knows; there's something reassuring about his poetry, they feel—almost like prose. Certainly there's nothing hard or odd or gloomy about it.

These views of Frost, it seems to me, come either from not knowing his poems well enough or from knowing the wrong poems too well. Frost's best-known poems, with a few exceptions, are not his best poems at all. [...]

So far from being obvious, optimistic, orthodox, many of [Frost's] poems are extraordinarily subtle and strange, poems which express an attitude that, at its most extreme, makes pessimism seem a hopeful evasion; they begin with a flat and terrible reproduction of the evil in the world and end by saying: It's so; and there's nothing you can do about it; and if there were, would *you* ever do it? The limits which existence approaches and falls back from have seldom been stated with such bare composure. [...]

The most awful of Frost's smaller poems is one called "Design" [...] This is the Argument from Design with a vengeance; is the terrible negative from which the eighteenth century's Kodak picture (with its *Having wonderful time. Wish you were here* on the margin) had to be printed. If a watch, then a watch-maker; if a diabolical machine, then a diabolical mechanic—Frost uses exactly the logic that has always been used. And this little albino catastrophe is too whitely catastrophic to be accidental, too impossibly unlikely ever to be a coincidence: accident, chance, statistics, natural selection are helpless to account for such designed terror and heartbreak, such an awful symbolic perversion of the innocent being of the world.

—Randall Jarrell, "The Other Frost" and "To the Laodiceans," *Poetry and the Age* (New York: Alfred A. Knopf, 1953) pp. 26–8, 42

LIONEL TRILLING ON FROST AS A "TERRIFYING POET"

[American literary and cultural critic Lionel Trilling (1905–1975) wrote several influential books, including *The Liberal Imagination* (1950), *The Opposing Self* (1955), and *Beyond Culture* (1965). Trilling's speech at the celebration of Frost's 85th birthday on March 26, 1959, triggered a series of rebuttals by people who considered Trilling's assessment an affront to Frost's venerable reputation.]

I have to say that my Frost—*my Frost*: what airs we give ourselves when once we believe that we have come into possession of a poet!—I have to say that my Frost is not the Frost I seem to perceive existing in the minds of so many of his admirers. He is not the Frost who confounds the characteristically modern practice of poetry by his notable democratic simplicity of utterance: on the contrary. He is not the Frost who controverts the bitter modern astonishment at the nature of human life: the opposite is so. He is not the Frost who reassures us by his affirmation of old virtues, simplicities, pieties, and ways of feeling: anything but. I will not go so far as to say that my Frost is not essentially an American poet at all: I believe that he is quite as American as everyone thinks he is, but not in the way everyone thinks he is. [. . .]

I conceive that Robert Frost is doing in his poems what [D. H.] Lawrence says the great writers of the classic American tradition did. That enterprise of theirs was of an ultimate radicalism. It consisted, Lawrence says, of two things: a disintegration and a sloughing off of the old consciousness, by which Lawrence means the old European consciousness, and the forming of a new consciousness underneath.

So radical a work, I need scarcely say, is not carried out by reassurance, nor by the affirmation of old virtues and pieties. It is carried out by the representation of the terrible actualities of life in a new way. I think of Frost as a terrifying poet. Call him, if it makes things any easier, a tragic poet, but it might be useful every now and then to come out from under the shelter of that literary word. The universe that he conceives is a terrifying universe. Read the poem called "Design" and see if you sleep the better for it. Read "Neither Out Far nor In Deep," which often seems to me the most perfect poem of our time, and see if you are warmed by anything in it except the energy with which the emptiness is perceived.

But the *people*, it will be objected, the *people* who inhabit this possibly terrifying universe! About them there is nothing that can terrify; surely the people in Mr. Frost's poems can only reassure us by their integrity and solidity. Perhaps so. But I cannot make the disjunction. It may well be that ultimately they reassure us in some sense, but first they terrify us, or should. We must not be misled about them by the curious tenderness with which they are represented, a tenderness which extends to a recognition of the tenderness they themselves can often give. But when ever have people been so isolated, so lightning-blasted, so tried down and calcined by life, so reduced, each in his own way, to some last irreducible core of being. Talk of the disintegration and sloughing off of the old consciousness! The people of Robert Frost's poems have done that with a vengeance.

—Lionel Trilling, "A Speech on Robert Frost: A Cultural Episode,"
Partisan Review 26, No. 3 (Summer 1959): 450-1

☙

MORDECAI MARCUS ON NATURAL EVIL AND THE ARGUMENT FROM "DESIGN"

[Mordecai Marcus is a professor of English at the University of Nebraska-Lincoln. This extract, from *The Poems of Robert Frost: An Explication* (1991), analyzes the poem's relation to literary and biblical discussions of divine control of nature.]

Interrupting the pattern of poems in which nature is gently ambiguous, "Design" suggests nature's terrifying potential for evil. Perhaps the most often initially misunderstood of Frost's poems, "Design" fools some readers because of its matter-of-factness and mock cheerfulness. Such interpretation sometimes persists in face of Frost's claim that he wrote the poem as an answer to William Cullen Bryant's famous nineteenth-century poem "To a Waterfowl," in which the speaker assures himself that both the perilous and distant flight of a bird and his own steps will be carefully guided by God. The poem rehearses the speaker's contemplative observation of an outdoor scene. On a white specimen of a normally blue flower, he sees an albino spider, whose fatness and whiteness parody the innocence of a baby, holding a dead moth. The moth is given falsely aesthetic qualities by being likened to a rigid piece of soft satin. Although these are indeed "Assorted characters of death and blight," they are immediately described as something cheerful—from the perspective of witches, for whom evil and horrifying brews of the normal are a delight. Randall Jarrell sees here a parody of breakfast-cereal advertisements.

With the seventh line, the tone starts to change. The speaker's normal, heartbroken response comes out almost straightforwardly in a condensed description, in which "snow-drop," "froth," and "paper kite" continue to mock and horrify. This voice that sinks toward despair takes a sharper descent with the second stanza's agonized questions. What, he asks, was appropriate about the color of purity and innocence as a backdrop for this small-scale murder? And why should a normally blue flower called the "heal-all" become a white camouflage for such an act? The questioning grows more sinister as he wonders what force had brought spider and moth together in the darkness. Toward the end, his questioning becomes rhetorical: he suggests that this tiny "design" might really be one of darkly evil forces. At the very end, he seems to pull back from his seriousness and suggest that perhaps there is no design on this unimportant level—that it governs only things closer to the human. Here he plays on the reader's self-concern, trickily contrasting it to the Bible's idea that God's eye is on the fall of the sparrow. Thus, if there is no design for small things, there can be none for larger ones. The poem alludes to the "argument from design," which says that if there is a design there must be a designer. The implication is that given such a terrifying and unjust example of design, the designer may be equally evil, or (as the very end of the poem suggests) nonexistent—for if there is no design for small things, perhaps there is none for anything. David Perkins argues that interpretations such as this are mistaken and that the poem is a "parody directed against a mock opponent," such as those who believe in the argument from design, a view Frost can't take seriously. Rather than arguing for the existence of demonic evil, then, Frost is just playing with the idea. This minority view may help explain why many readers of the poem do not share the speaker's apparent horror at the scene.

—Mordecai Marcus, *The Poems of Robert Frost: An Explication*
(Boston: G. K. Hall & Co., 1991), pp. 152-3

[George F. Bagby teaches at Hampden-Sydney College and is the author of *Frost and the Book of Nature* (1993), from which this extract is taken. Bagby explores Frost's debt to Ralph Waldo Emerson (1803–1882) and examines his use of the long-standing literary and philosophical trope of the natural world as a "text" that can be read for evidence of the divine or spiritual.]

Frost seems to be harking back to a displaced version of the (ultimately Augustinian) notion of *vestigia Dei*, the "footprints" or "traces" of God in the created world. [...]

[An] important instance of this sort of metaphor occurs in "Design," where Frost calls the flower, spider, and moth "Assorted characters of death and blight." "Characters" is doubly metaphorical: it sees these three things not only as living presences, *dramatis personae*, but also as letters in a message that the poet must decipher. Or again, echoing one of Whitman's favorite wordplays, "leaves" in the sense of foliage are also pages in the vegetable text: fossilized remains, which Frost calls "leaves of stone," are "The picture book of the trilobite," an age-old natural encyclopedia.

In itself no one of these instances would be greatly significant, perhaps; but cumulatively, all of these (and other) plays on and metaphors of "print" and "characters" and "leaves" surely project an implicit view of the created world as a kind of text. [...]

But again, as in the case of correspondences, the crucial metaphor of nature as a text of revelation is transmitted from the seventeenth century to Frost chiefly through Emerson and Thoreau. Emerson, as usual, formulates the idea more systematically: "Nature is language & every new fact that we learn is a new word; but rightly seen, taken all together it is not merely a language but the language put together into a most significant & universal book. I wish to learn the language not that I may know a new set of nouns & verbs but that I may read the great book which is written in that tongue."

The sources of the metaphor are suggested with unusual clarity in the most explicit version of it in Frost's poetry, in that important sonnet "Time Out." The wanderer, as we have seen, pauses and realizes:

> The mountain he was climbing had the slant
> As of a book held up before his eyes
> (And was a text albeit done in plant).
> Dwarf cornel, goldthread, and *Maianthemum*,
> He followingly fingered as he read . . .

Given the fact that this poem was probably written in 1939, the archaism of the crucial parenthetical line— "(And was a text albeit done in plant)"—amounts almost to a bow to the venerable tradition that descends from the seventeenth century. But the last two quoted lines show clearly how that tradition has been filtered through Frost's nineteenth-century American forebears: both the naturalist's attention to the species of plant involved and the hands-on "fingering" of those plants represent Frost at his most Thoreauvian.

—George F. Bagby, *Frost and the Book of Nature* (Knoxville: University of Tennessee Press, 1993), pp. 9–11

❦

EDWARD J. INGEBRETSEN ON RELIGIOUS TERROR IN "DESIGN"

[Edward J. Ingebretsen, a professor of literature at Georgetown University, is a member of the executive committee of the Robert Frost Society and the author of several articles on Frost and American literature. In this extract, Ingebretsen compares "Design" to Jonathan Edwards's (1703–1758) "Sinners in the Hands of an Angry God."]

Reflect for a moment on Edwards's sermon, "Sinners in the Hands of an Angry God," and Frost's "Design." "Design," distant, studiedly formal, reveals the ambiguity of Frost's metaphor: the design that frees, can, by overdesigning, trap. Similarly, in his private life Frost found that the religious bent of his imagination accorded him the terror of a too-orderly Newtonian universe while lacking any of its rhetorical consolations. That the universe has a design is of no comfort if it is designed with your torment in mind. One understands why Trilling found the poem didn't make for easy sleeping: "What but design of darkness to appall? / If design govern in a thing so small." Yet, the world of "Design" is not too distant from the universe of "Sinners in the Hands of an Angry God." In both cases entrapment results in anger, terror and passivity—surely a parody of the self-effacing awe one typically expected in the presence of the Divine. Frost increases Edwards's sense of help-lessness while sharpening his own irony, since the minister's spider—a metaphor for the victim of judgment—in "Design" becomes judgment's unwitting agent. Edwards imagines God holding the sinner like a spider over the fire. Frost, however, mutes the melodrama, perhaps with the purpose of freeing God from responsibility. He more soberly includes the spider, making it part of the tableaux. Nonetheless, both sermon and poem present designs "of darkness to appall." Edwards' terror seems because of God—dying under the judgment of God; for Frost the terror, rather, seems *despite* God—living under the judgment of life, enduring what he called "the Trial by Existence." However, the two artists can only be compared so far. Frost, the modernist, realized better than Edwards the aesthetic limits of language. He under-stood the consequences—limits—of his metaphors: "All metaphor breaks down somewhere. That is the beauty of it." So Frost suc-ceeded only partially in freeing himself from the terms employed by Edwards and bequeathed to him by John Calvin.

—Edward J. Ingebretsen, "'Design of darkness to appall': Religious Terror in the Poetry of Robert Frost," *The Robert Frost Review* (1993): 53–4, 56

⊕

JOSEPH BRODSKY ON NATURE AS A SELF-PORTRAIT

[Joseph Brodsky (1940–1996), a Russian-born poet and essayist, became a U.S. citizen in 1977. He was awarded the Nobel Prize for literature in 1987. In this extract, from an essay written 35 years after Trilling's 1959 speech,

Brodsky revisits the controversy to clarify terms and offer his own response to the view of Frost as "homespun Yankee nature bard."]

In 1959, at a banquet thrown in New York on the occasion of Robert Frost's eighty-fifth birthday, the most prominent literary critic at that time, Lionel Trilling, rose and declared that Robert Frost was "a terrifying poet." That, of course, caused a certain stir, but the epithet was well chosen.

Now, I want you to make the distinction here between terrifying and tragic. Tragedy, as you know, is always a fait accompli, whereas terror always has to do with anticipation, with man's recognition of his own negative potential—with his sense of what he is capable of. And it is the latter that was Frost's forte, not the former. In other words, his posture is radically different from the Continental tradition of the poet as tragic hero. And that difference alone makes him—for want of a better term—American.

On the surface, he looks very positively predisposed toward his surroundings—particularly toward nature. His fluency, his "being versed in country things" alone can produce this impression. However, there is a difference between the way a European perceives nature and the way an American does. Addressing this difference, W. H. Auden, in his short essay on Frost, suggests something to the effect that when a European conceives of confronting nature, he walks out of his cottage or a little inn, filled with either friends or family, and goes for an evening stroll. If he encounters a tree, it's a tree made familiar by history, to which it's been a witness. This or that king sat underneath it, laying down this or that law—something of that sort. A tree stands there rustling, as it were, with allusions. Pleased and somewhat pensive, our man, refreshed but unchanged by that encounter, returns to his inn or cottage, finds his friends or family absolutely intact, and proceeds to have a good, merry time. Whereas when an American walks out of his house and encounters a tree it is a meeting of equals. Man and tree face each other in their respective primal power, free of references: neither has a past, and as to whose future is greater, it is a toss-up. Basically, it's epidermis meeting bark. Our man returns to his cabin in a state of bewilderment, to say the least, if not in actual shock or terror.

Now, this is obviously a romantic caricature, but it accentuates the features, and that's what I am after here. In any case, the second point could be safely billed as the gist of Robert Frost's nature poetry. Nature for this poet is neither friend nor foe, nor is it the backdrop for human drama; it is this poet's terrifying self-portrait.

—Joseph Brodsky, "On Grief and Reason," *The New Yorker* (September 26, 1994): 70–2

Thematic Analysis of
"Directive"
(including a discussion of
"Stopping by the Woods on a Snowy Evening")

"Directive," from *Steeple Bush* (1947), has been called Frost's single best poem, demonstrating the height of his unique canniness and insight. Tonally varied throughout, it fluctuates between archness and ruggedness, poignancy and bitterness. Not as friendly as readers often expect Frost's work to be, "Directive" bristles and resists easy interpretation, but it is precisely this uneasiness about its scene and its subject that conveys a moving view of human loss.

A "directive" is an authoritative statement of advice or instruction. The word was more commonly used in the nineteenth century for the directions that describe the route to a hard-to-find place, and Frost's "directive" points to a hidden place indeed. The speaker returns to the scene of an abandoned farm, now overgrown, that is part of a town that has also been deserted and reabsorbed into the woods.

The retreat into the "backcountry" is a movement backward in place and in time. The poem begins abruptly "Back out of all this now too much for us," echoing a sonnet by William Wordsworth (1770–1850), "The World Is Too Much with Us." In Wordsworth's poem, the speaker describes how ". . .we lay waste our powers;/Little we see in Nature that is ours,/We have given our hearts away, a sordid boon." Frost picks up Wordsworth's concern with nature "dispossessing" us and flouting human efforts. Wordsworth goes on to describe the landscape and long for a lost mythological past to mollify his sense of alienation, and Frost undertakes a similar procedure, turning to reconsider lost mythologies. Yet Frost is far more bitter and ironic, even ruthless, about such attempts to "pick up the pieces."

The speaker also moves "back in a time made simple by the loss/of detail." "Simple" here does not imply a pleasant freedom from complexity but a frustrating sense of "simple" as "stupid." The scene has been dumbed down, as well as muted, by a natural world that is resistant to human markers. Humanly inscribed detail has been "burned, dissolved, and broken off," exemplified in the weathered "graveyard marble." This image presents the paradox of human memorials: Even monuments erected to perpetuate a memory are subject to disintegration. As human artifacts are made "meaningless," human language is also subject to an evacuation of sense. Frost makes three paradoxical statements: "There is a house that is no more a house/Upon a farm that is no more a farm/And in a town that is no more a town." As the poet names them, these things are what they are not. Human acts of naming do not in any way alter their fate.

The poem offers a despairing, ironic account of a failed attempt at farming. The former homestead is now a ruin. Tracing the way back to it, Frost introduces the figure of a guide "who only has at heart your getting lost." Deliberate misdirection of a quest has important literary antecedents that Frost likely had in mind, including Edmund Spenser's (ca. 1552–1599) *The Faerie Queene*, Book I and Robert Browning's (1812–1889) "Childe Roland to the Dark Tower Came." In Browning's poem, the guide is there to "waylay with his lies," but the questor finds his way to a landscape that Frost's scene strikingly recalls: in "starved ignoble nature," "penury, inertness and grimace,/In some strange sort, were the land's portion" (lines 56, 61–62).

Frost describes this unfriendly landscape as having the *body* of a powerful adversary. The rocky terrain of Panther Mountain is personified with "monolithic *knees*." The glacier "braced its *feet* against the Arctic Pole." The cedar tree has an "instep arch." These images anthropomorphize nature but only to suggest far greater physical force than a human body can muster. Nature has succeeded in ousting the human inhabitants, reclaiming what human agency had tried in vain to claim.

The returning visitor is watched by "eye pairs out of forty firkins" (a "firkin" is a small wooden tub). The "upstart inexperience" of the curious animals recalls the inexperience of the farm's former *human* inhabitants, a hopeful perspective that has since been shattered. The speaker bitterly mocks the achievement of having "shaded out/A few old pecker-fretted apple trees," keenly aware of the impotence of his own attempt to settle there.

Aware of his own projections on the scene, the speaker advises, "Make yourself up a cheering song." The poem can be read as an attempt at that "cheering song" that knows itself to be unsuccessfully cheerful. Despite its wry humor, the poem never dispels the gloom of exile. The word "lost" reappears, implying both directional "getting lost" and psychological loss, and both senses are mapped together as a kind of secularized parable that we cannot be sure how to interpret. The speaker stumbles upon the children's playhouse, which comes to represent a lost state of joy, and bids us to "Weep for what little things could make them glad." This kind of easy "gladness" is now impossible. The playhouse image is immediately contrasted by the horrifying picture of "a house in earnest," its cellar hole "slowly closing like a dent in dough," a homely emblem of annihilation and nothingness: human habitation has been consumed in the savage and unappeasable forces of nature. The message of this "parable" seems to be that in the end, entropy wins.

In the poem's final movement, beginning with line 49, the speaker yearns for "sacramental" significance in this "pilgrimage." He finds the brook he was looking for, and deliberately assigns it a metaphorical value as "your destiny." The poem suggests that the speaker *wishes* the brook could be an "original" source to reconnect him with his "origins," but knows it cannot.

The speaker finds a "broken goblet like the Grail," but this explicit invocation of an idea of romantic quest is immediately juxtaposed with another reference that ironizes and transforms it. The goblet has been hidden "so the wrong ones can't find it,/So can't get saved," a reference to the Gospel of Mark (4:11–12), in which Jesus tells the apostles that "those who are outside . . . may look and look, but see nothing; they may listen and listen, but understand nothing." Frost's poem takes up the question of who is permitted understanding, who is or is not excluded from salvation, and he builds the question into the poem in a complicated way. Frost points out the most callous and exclusionary interpretation possible for this text, the elitist sense that "wrong ones" are denied salvation. Critics have debated the relation of this allusion to the rest of the poem, but however we judge its significance, it reflects the poem's strong sense that if there ever was a covenant for this speaker, it has failed.

The speaker of the poem watches himself closely as he goes to take a supposedly restorative drink. In this self-consciousness, this poem exemplifies a tendency in Frost's poetry for the surface to take you in several different directions at once, an apparent simplicity that is not simple at all. The poem's final line is especially ambiguous. The speaker issues the imperative "Drink and be whole again beyond confusion." Does "beyond confusion" suggest a state of *clarity* that can be attained by drinking the waters? Or is "beyond confusion" a state of confusion in the extreme (as one might say, "this problem is beyond confusing")? Is the line ironic, conscious of the futility of any such sacramental attempts to "drink and be whole"? The poem ends with an ought-to-have-been epiphany that is not a moment of clarification at all but a moment of deeper ambivalence and uncertainty.

Frost addresses the very question of how to make poetic use of a moment like this at all. As his allusions suggest, he explores the significance of any literary effort to console or explain. The poem becomes an act of "taking stock" of poetry. Frost wrote that poetry functions as "a momentary stay against confusion" and in this poem he questions this capacity. An older Frost (age 73 at the time of *Steeple Bush*'s publication) seems to be speaking to his younger, more hopeful self, not only about farming but about writing. He implies an uncomfortable examination of the power and utility of his own art: What good has poetry been to me? What use is it to anybody? Why bother writing poems about experiences of loss? In "Directive," the experiential loss does not add up to any imaginative gain. Nothing has been cleared up. And yet the poem has been written, testament to the difficulty of its making.

In "Directive," the speaker of the poem is "stopping by the woods" to contemplate the inhospitable depths of an inhuman wilderness. A poem more frequently anthologized as an example of this kind of dark ambivalence in the face of nature is Frost's much earlier "Stopping by the Woods on a Snowy Evening," from *New Hampshire* (1923). As snow fills up the woods, it covers and muffles evidence of human presence, and the solitary speaker finds himself seduced by the utter stillness. Stopping far from civilization, the speaker pauses for an unusual anti-ritual in his routine travels, beckoned by the woods' sublimity. When the horse "gives his harness bells a shake/To ask if there is some mistake," he stands for civilization, keeping the speaker from his isolation and signaling in a simple, interrogative "language." But the terrifying lightness of sight and sound leads the speaker to contemplate the woods as "lovely, dark, and deep," a desire to lose himself in this self-annihilating scene. In the final lines, which many have interpreted as a turning away from the wish to commit suicide, the speaker resists the urge to succumb to the woods' life-extinguishing power, remembering the "promises" he has made to the world of the village and farmhouse ahead of him. The repetition of "And miles to go before I sleep" gives the phrase a somber cadence and enforces its figurative meaning: The speaker has far to travel on the road that evening, and also far to go in his life's travel and travail before the sleep of death. ❀

Critical Views on
"Directive"

ROBERT FROST ON "THE FIGURE A POEM MAKES"

[Frost's 1939 edition of his *Collected Poems* carried an introductory essay, from which this extract is taken. Frost included the essay in several later collections of his work, and it is often quoted as an *ars poetica*, setting forth his precepts for poetry. The last line of "Directive" echoes its description of poetry as "a momentary stay against confusion."]

It should be of the pleasure of the poem itself to tell how it can [fulfill its subject]. The figure a poem makes. It begins in delight and ends in wisdom. The figure is the same as for love. No one can really hold that the ecstasy should be static and stand still in one place. It begins in delight, it inclines to the impulse, it assumes direction with the first line laid down, it runs a course of lucky events, and ends in a clarification of life—not necessarily a great clarification, such as sects and cults are founded on, but in a momentary stay against confusion. It has denouement. It has an outcome that though unforeseen was predestined from the first image of the original mood—and indeed from the very mood. It is but a trick poem and no poem at all if the best of it was thought of first and saved for the last. It finds its own name as it goes and discovers the best waiting for it in some final phrase at once wise and sad—the happy-sad blend of the drinking song.

No tears in the writer, no tears in the reader. No surprise for the writer, no surprise for the reader. For me the initial delight is in the surprise of remembering something I didn't know I knew. I am in a place, in a situation, as if I had materialized from cloud or risen out of the ground. There is a glad recognition of the long lost and the rest follows. Step by step the wonder of the unexpected supply keeps growing. The impressions most useful to my purpose seem always those I was unaware of and so made no note of at the time when taken, and the conclusion is come to that like giants we are always hurling experience ahead of us to pave the future with against the day when we may want to strike a line of purpose across it for somewhere. The line will have the more charm for not being mechanically straight. We enjoy the straight crookedness of a good walking stick. Modern instruments of precision are being used to make things crooked as if by eye and hand in the old days. [...]

More than once I should have lost my soul to radicalism if it had been the originality it was mistaken for by its young converts. Originality and initiative are what I ask for my country. For myself the originality need be no more than the freshness of a poem run in the way I have described: from delight to wisdom. The figure is the same as for love. Like a piece of ice on a hot stove the poem must ride on its own melting. A poem may be worked over once it is in being, but may not be worried into being. Its most precious quality will remain its having run itself and carried away the poet with it. Read it a hundred times: it will forever keep its freshness as a metal keeps its fragrance. It can never lose its sense of a meaning that once unfolded by surprise as it went.

—Robert Frost, "The Figure a Poem Makes," *Robert Frost: Poetry and Prose*, ed. Edward C. Lathem and Lawrance Thompson (New York: Holt, Rinehart and Winston, 1972), pp. 394–5, 396

©

W. H. AUDEN ON LANDSCAPE, RUIN, AND POETIC TEMPERAMENT

[W. H. Auden (1907–1973) was an English-born poet, playwright, and man of letters who settled in the United States in 1939 and became a U.S. citizen. He was known for his concern with social realities and leftist politics, and later for his commitment to High-Church Christianity. His poems are gathered in *Collected Shorter Poems* 1927–57 (1967) and *Collected Longer Poems* (1969), and his prose in *The Enchafed Flood* (1950) and *The Dyer's Hand* (1962), from which this extract is taken. In this essay on Frost, he observes that poetry seeks "clarification" through a poet's unique confrontation with landscape.]

Any poetry which aims at being a clarification of life must be concerned with two questions about which all men, whether they read poetry or not, seek clarification.

1. *Who am I?* What is the difference between man and all other creatures? What relations are possible between them? What is man's status in the universe? What are the conditions of his existence which he must accept as his fate which no wishing can alter?

2. *Whom ought I to become?* What are the characteristics of the hero, the authentic man whom everybody should admire and try to become? Vice versa, what are the characteristics of the churl, the unauthentic man whom everybody should try to avoid becoming?

We all seek answers to these questions which shall be universally valid under all circumstances, but the experiences to which we put them are always local both in time and place. What any poet has to say about man's status in nature, for example, depends in part upon the landscape and climate he happens to live in and in part upon the reactions to it of his personal temperament. A poet brought up in the tropics cannot have the same vision as a poet brought up in Hertfordshire and, if they inhabit the same landscape, the chirpy social endomorph will give a different picture of it from that of the melancholic withdrawn ectomorph.

The nature of Frost's poetry is the nature of New England. New England is made of granite, is mountainous, densely wooded, and its soil is poor. It has a long severe winter, a summer that is milder and more pleasant than in most parts of the States, a short and sudden spring, a slow and theatrically beautiful fall. Since it adjoins the eastern seaboard, it was one of the first areas to be settled but, as soon as the more fertile lands to the West were opened up, it began to lose population. Tourists and city dwellers who can afford a summer home may arrive for the summer, but much land which was once cultivated has gone back to the wild.

One of Frost's favorite images is the image of the abandoned house. In Britain or Europe, a ruin recalls either historical change, political acts like war or enclosure, or, in the case of abandoned mine buildings, a successful past which came to an end, not because nature was too strong, but because she had been robbed of everything she possessed. A ruin in Europe, therefore, tends to arouse reflections about human injustice and greed and the nemesis that overtakes human pride. But in Frost's poetry, a ruin is an image of human heroism, of a defense in the narrow pass against hopeless odds.

—W. H. Auden, "Robert Frost," *The Dyer's Hand and Other Essays* (New York: Random House, 1962), pp. 344–5

MARIE BORROFF ON THE NEW TESTAMENT ALLUSION IN "DIRECTIVE"

[Marie Borroff is Professor Emeritus of English at Yale University. Her critical works include *Sir Gawain and the Green Knight: A Stylistic and Metrical Study* (1962) and *Language and the Poet: Verbal Artistry in Frost, Stevens, and Moore* (1979), from which this extract is taken. Borroff addresses Frost's alienating pose in adapting this biblical text to the poem.]

The passage in Mark identifying the "wrong ones," those who will not be able to find the goblet, makes it clear that the salvation promised at the end of the poem is available only to those who understand what is said in "parables." If by a parable we mean a story in which things and actions are to be interpreted symbolically, differing from allegory not so much in the formal relationship between literal and symbolic as in the homely and everyday character of its subject matter and its emphasis upon the moral qualities of human action, then poems like "Mending Wall," "Mowing," "Hyla Brook," and others discussed above are, precisely, parables. So too is the conclusion of "Directive." Only if we understand the symbolic significance of the ritual will we receive its saving moral message: only in the imagination capable of understanding these symbols is the "good ground" on which the message will bear fruit. Yet the message itself, it must be insisted, is not Christian. The revelation the poem brings is moral rather than supernatural; its source is not a divine incarnation but a secular figure, the poet, who, although his garments may resemble the priest's, belongs to the realm of human experience and memory. Despite his exploitation of the Christian tradition in the structure, symbolism, and language of his poems, the supreme bearer of spiritual enlightenment in our time, for Frost, was poetry itself. The last line of "Directive," as S. P. C. Duvall has pointed out, is reminiscent of the poet's famous definition of poetry as "a momentary stay against confusion."

In setting himself up as the exclusive "guide" ("And put a sign up CLOSED to all but me") to a truth he has hedged about with verbal and symbolic obscurities, and in proceeding to imply that only those who can interpret this poetically mediated truth are worthy to be saved, Frost, one may well think, has his nerve. The teasing and testing, the archness and complacent whimsy, will always alienate a certain number of readers, and long familiarity will not render them any less irritating. But though "Directive" is flawed in part by the arch-avuncular pose of the elderly Frost, it is not seriously damaged. The ideal it upholds—the encompassing of Puritanical grimness and strength by a saving joy and imagination—is powerful and viable in this as in the other poems which make up Frost's New Testament. And, in "Directive" particularly, we must admire the brilliance with which so great a range of resources—rural Americana, American-style humorous understatement, legend, history and fairy tale, the literary past, the chivalric and Christian traditions—has been drawn upon and forged into a stylistic whole. Here, as in all Frost's best poems, what is literary and elevated seems not to impose itself upon, but to rise naturally from, basic simplicity—the everyday things of country life, lucidly and concretely rendered in common language— which is Frost's primary and most memorable poetic world.

—Marie Borroff, *Language and the Poet: Verbal Artistry in Frost, Stevens, and Moore* (Chicago: University of Chicago Press, 1979), pp. 40–1

❧

SYDNEY LEA ON FROST'S RELATION TO WORDSWORTH

[Sydney Lea is a professor of English at the University of Massachusetts and editor of the *New England Review* and *Breadloaf Quarterly*. He is the author of several critical articles and books of poems. In this extract, Lea compares Frost's stance of "playing" at the sublime to Wordsworth's "egotistical sublime," the assertion that "mind and world could interfuse."]

What, then, was the influence Frost felt? Simply, not a so-called Romantic one: indeed, Frost comes closest to direct tribute in remarks on "Ode to Duty," in which Wordsworth discards his own "Romanticism." It is this disenchanted poet who informs Frost's work, but Frost (with real acuteness) had heard the disenchanted voice even in the assured poetry of Wordsworth's egotistical sublime. In this essay I will try to read Wordsworth's poems as Frost did, for Frost's canon may be seen as a purgation of Wordsworth's, "dropping" below his predecessor's in more than stylistic ways, dispelling even the vestigial illusions, as Frost views them, of the chastened Wordsworth. As we shall see, it displaces Imagination with *Fancy* (or "Yankee" skepticism: unwillingness to suspend belief, wit, or reason). Pastoral retreat concomitantly collapses into stingy timbered-land, belief in a possible sublime into stubborn earthiness, poem as redemption into poem as "rigamarole." [...]

Against all this [Wordsworth's influence], the very particularism of Frost, his tendency in "Directive" and generally to earthward, is the clearer. What I now will urge is how small in him is the capacity for the sublime. He presents a falling, not of starry wonder into landscape, but of word into empty prospects and imagination into tentative fancy, so that there is rarely a *feeling* analogous to the supernatural in his work but only a playing at it.

What, though, of the final directive of "Directive," "Drink and be whole again beyond confusion"? The phrase inevitably summons Frost's famous "figure a poem makes": "It ends in a clarification—not necessarily a great clarification, such as sects and cults are founded on, but a momentary stay against confusion." Yet I have insisted, despite the idealizers, that such clarification is based on disenchanted perception, on desublimization. There is nothing in this figure but figuration, nothing either in "Directive" beyond the moment: indeed, the return to a source in this work may be a return to the capacity of seeing object-as-object, may be a clearing away of complex affective obstacles to gladness, like the children's, at little things.

If Wordsworth asserted that mind and world could interfuse, that their cooperative accomplishment was so mighty as to merit no lower name than creation, Frost in his run-out landscape offers precisely a lowering of poetic claims in general. Little things remain little, for he has neither means nor intention to make great things of the small, in the manner of Wordsworth's so-called "higher minds."

—Sydney Lea, "From Sublime to Rigamarole: Relations of Frost to Wordsworth," *Studies in Romanticism* 19 (1980): 84, 103

☙

HERBERT MARKS ON THE POEM AS PARABLE

[Herbert Marks is an associate professor of comparative literature and religious studies at Indiana University. He is the author of several essays on the Bible in modern literature. In this extract, Marks analyzes, in light of several of Frost's poems, how "Directive" can be construed either as offering "sacramental" conviction or as presenting only the certainty of fragmentation.]

Like the Gospel parables themselves, "Directive" can be read in two ways. It can be interpreted point for point (allegorically); or it can be construed in its entirety as illustrating a single conviction (the way form criticism insists Jesus' parables were originally meant to be taken). The latter approach suggests an alternative to the sacramental reading of the poem; for search as we may, the only integrating conviction—the only common term between Frost's poem and experience—is the certainty of fragmentation. That is, read as parable, the poem invites us to achieve the only wholeness possible by becoming reconciled to the imperfect. It offers us a road—later called a ladder—that "may seem as if it should have been a quarry," glacial etchings in the rock, cellar holes, a field eroded to the size of a harness gall, and, in its midst, a "children's house of make believe," with some "shattered dishes" and the broken goblet used to draw the water. These analects become more meaningful when read with an eye to their individual histories—especially in Frost's own poems. Thus, if we move to an "allegorical" reading, the "ladder road" recalls the two-pointed ladder of metaphor that points toward heaven in "After Apple Picking"; the glacier "that braced his feet against the Arctic Pole" is a manifestation or emissary of the same elusive unnameable that haunts the polar mind in "An Empty Threat"; and the traces it leaves on the ledges run "southeast northwest" by reason of the same imaginative westering that makes all "zest/To materialize/By on-penetration" run in the same direction in "Kitty Hawk."

This fragmentary style of reference seems especially fitting in a poem that would vindicate process. As Frost writes in "The Prerequisites," "A poem is best read in light of all the other poems ever written. We read A the better to read B. . . . Progress is not the aim, but circulation." Moreover, his determination in "The Lesson for Today," to "take [his] incompleteness with the rest," shows that he recognized the limitations of the approach. And yet a close explicator could still argue that the aim of "Directive" is to transcend and so perfect its fragments: that the counterplot I have been tracing is only its *praeparatio evangelica*. The final question is thus whether "the road there," so similar to the dialectical path of the quest romance, leads to some determinate source, or whether our gift at journey's end is just the preacher's vexing wisdom. Does one really come back to the original word or only to another departure?

The answer hinges on our reading of the final phrase, "beyond confusion." The word "confusion" occurs frequently in Frost's work, where it usually connotes disorder and defeat. The reference to the confusion of Babel in Frost's letter to Cox, for example, and the description of "the background in hugeness and confusion shading away from where we stand into black and utter chaos" in his letter to *The Amherst Student* both depend on this usage. If this is the only sense intended in "Directive," then the final line exceeds without question Frost's own definition of a poem's end as "a momentary stay against confusion."

—Herbert Marks, "The Counter-Intelligence of Robert Frost," *The Yale Review* 71 (1982): 574–6

CHARLES BERGER ON RETURNING TO ORIGINS

[Charles Berger is a professor of English at the University of Utah and the author of *Forms of Farewell: The Late Poetry of*

Wallace Stevens (1985). In this extract, Berger interprets "Directive" as offering a riddling commentary on its retreat into the past.]

From the beginning of "Directive" the movement back toward an earlier time is viewed as a return to simplicity, in the root sense of oneness, that which is not compounded or confused, to draw on the poem's last word. To go back behind—or beyond—confusion is to return to the unity of wholeness. This movement, from the beginning, is seen as a fashioned action— "a time made simple"—and a violent one as well. The simple thing, here at the beginning, is seen not so much as totality, but as a synecdoche, a microcosm. Wholeness is not achieved without the violence of prior fragmentation. And the word "simple" of course carries its negative connotations as well, so that the loss of detail could lead to a damning as well as a saving simplicity, could lead to forgetfulness as much as remembrance. Simplicity here is achieved through the loss of what Frost terms "detail," a word that can be taken in a number of contexts, either as richness or as superfluity. How much of a loss *is* the loss of detail.

And this action of burning, dissolving, breaking off—is it healing violence, a counter-violence aimed against the wounds of the past? Even before Frost reaches the series of famous paradoxes—"a house that is no more a house . . . "—the poem is riddled with dark sayings about the nature of this regenerative turn to the simple past, filled with the poet's sense of the double nature of what he is doing even as he asserts the triumph of the *simplex*, the single thing that can save us.

Despite its emphasis on wholeness and simplicity, "Directive" also has a kind of division built into it in the form of the split between the narrating guide and his audience. "Let us go then, you and I," goes the poem's implicit beginning; and the poem's action needs an auditor, an interpreter, an other, present at the site, to complete its meaning. One of the poem's many open questions is whether or not narrator and auditor merge at the close in the shared gesture of drinking the waters of the source. The offer is certainly made, but whether or not it is accepted depends upon the reaction of the reader-initiate. Equally unclear is whether the narrator drinks. Is he a guide whose mission is to lead others to a sacred spot he himself is barred from knowing? Or has he already tasted the waters? Poetic tradition certainly offers examples of guides, such as Virgil, or the

Ancient Mariner, who can save others but not themselves. One way of saving others is to warn them against the sins of the guide, and in this sense it is worth thinking about the narrator's implication in the scene of ruin he brings us to face. For this site in the woods may also be thought of as a scene of the crime. Indeed, if the allusion to St. Mark's cryptic passage points to the necessity of interpreting parables, then surely one of the poem's prime riddles is what connection can this speaker have to the landscape. To leave the house as merely a generalized example of human decay would seem to solve the riddle too quickly. Why does this speaker take us here? Why is he the only survivor of this house? Where is everyone else? Without joining the biographical debate over Frost's character, I find it perplexing that commentators have not called attention to the ruin of Frost's own "house" in treating the site of "Directive." The grim line "This was no playhouse but a house in earnest" seems to lose all resonance otherwise. Here we have "Home Burial" carried to the extreme: the home, "now slowly closing like a dent in dough," is being buried before our eyes.

> —Charles Berger, "Echoing Eden: Frost and Origins," *Robert Frost*, ed. Harold Bloom (New York: Chelsea House, 1986), pp. 161–2

Works by
Robert Frost

A Boy's Will. 1913.

North of Boston. 1914.

Mountain Interval. 1916.

New Hampshire. 1923.

Selected Poems. 1923, 1928, 1934, 1936, 1955, 1963.

West-Running Brook. 1928.

Collected Poems. 1930, 1939, 1946.

A Further Range. 1936.

A Witness Tree. 1942.

A Masque of Reason. 1945.

A Masque of Mercy. 1947.

Steeple Bush. 1947.

Complete Poems of Robert Frost. 1949.

Aforesaid. 1954.

In the Clearing. 1962.

The Poetry of Robert Frost: The Collected Poems, Complete and Unabridged. 1969.

Collected Poems, Prose, and Plays. 1995.

Works about Robert Frost

Auden, W. H. "Robert Frost." *The Dyer's Hand and Other Essays.* New York: Random House, 1962.

Bagby, George F. *Frost and the Book of Nature.* Knoxville: University of Tennessee Press, 1993.

Bloom, Harold, ed. *Robert Frost.* New York: Chelsea House, 1986.

Blum, Margaret. "Robert Frost's 'Directive': A Theological Reading." *Modern Language Notes* 76 (1961): 524–5.

Borroff, Marie. *Language and the Poet: Verbal Artistry in Frost, Stevens, and Moore.* Chicago: University of Chicago Press, 1979.

Brodsky, Joseph. "On Grief and Reason." *The New Yorker* (September 26, 1994): 70–5.

Cox, James. M., ed. *Robert Frost: A Collection of Critical Essays.* Englewood Cliffs, N.J.: Prentice-Hall, 1962.

Cox, Sidney. *A Swinger of Birches.* New York: New York University Press, 1960.

Donoghue, Denis. "Robert Frost." In *Connoisseurs of Chaos: Ideas of Order in Modern American Poetry.* New York: Macmillan, 1965.

Duvall, S. P. C. "Robert Frost's 'Directive' out of Walden." *American Literature* 31 (1960): 480–8.

Ellis, James. "Robert Frost's Four Types of Belief in 'Birches.'" *Robert Frost Review* (1993): 70–4.

Frost, Robert. *Robert Frost: Poetry and Prose.* Ed. Edward C. Lathem and Lawrance Thompson. New York: Holt, Rinehart and Winston, 1972.

George, William. "Frost's 'The Road Not Taken.'" *The Explicator* 49. No. 4 (1991):230–2.

Greenberg, Robert A., and James G. Hepburn, eds. *Robert Frost: An Introduction.* New York: Holt, Rinehart, and Winston, 1961.

Ingebretsen, Edward J. "'Design of darkness to appall': Religious Terror in the Poetry of Robert Frost." *Robert Frost Review* (1993): 50–7.

Jarrell, Randall. "The Other Frost" and "To the Laodiceans." In *Poetry and the Age.* New York: Alfred A. Knopf, 1953.

Kearns, Katherine. *Robert Frost and a Poetics of Appetite*. New York: Cambridge University Press, 1994.

Kennedy, John F. "Poetry and Power." *Atlantic Monthly* 213 (February 1964): 53–4.

Lea, Sydney. "From Sublime to Rigamarole: Relations of Frost to Wordsworth." *Studies in Romanticism* 19 (1980): 83–108.

Lentricchia, Frank. *Robert Frost: Modern Poetics and the Landscapes of Self*. Durham, N.C.: Duke University Press, 1975.

LeVay, John. "Frost's 'Directive.'" *The Explicator* 52. No. 1 (Fall 1993): 42–4.

Lowell, Amy. "North of Boston." *New Republic* 11 (February 20, 1915), 81–2.

Lynen, John F. *The Pastoral Art of Robert Frost*. New Haven: Yale University Press, 1960.

Marcus, Mordecai. *The Poems of Robert Frost: An Explication*. Boston: G. K. Hall & Co., 1991.

Marks, Herbert. "The Counter-Intelligence of Robert Frost." *Yale Review* 71 (1982): 554–8.

Maxson, H. A. *On the Sonnets of Robert Frost*. Jefferson, N.C.: McFarland & Co, 1997.

Meyer, Jeffrey. *Robert Frost: A Biography*. Boston: Houghton Mifflin, 1996.

Pack, Robert. "Frost's Enigmatical Reserve: The Poet as Teacher and Preacher." In *Affirming Limits: Essays on Mortality, Choice and Poetic Form*, 174–88. Amherst: University of Massachusetts Press, 1985.

Parfitt, Matthew. "Robert Frost's 'Modern Georgics.'" *Robert Frost Review* (1996): 54–70.

Poirier, Richard. *Robert Frost: The Work of Knowing*. New York: Oxford University Press, 1977.

Pound, Ezra. "*Review of North of Boston.*" *Poetry* 5. NO. 3 (December 1914): 127–30.

Pritchard, William. *Frost: A Literary Life Reconsidered*. New York: Oxford University Press, 1984.

Rotella, Guy. "Metaphor in Frost's 'Oven Bird.'" In *Robert Frost: The Man and the Poet*. Ed. Earl J. Wilcox. Rock Hill, S.C.: Winthrop Studies on Major Modern Writers, 1981.

Ryan, Alvan S. "Frost and Emerson: Voice and Vision." *Massachusetts Review* 1 (1959): 5–23.

Thompson, Lawrance. *Fire and Ice: The Art and Thought of Robert Frost.* New York: Holt, Rinehart, and Winston, 1942.

———. *Robert Frost: The Early Years,* 1874–1915. New York: Holt, Rinehart, and Winston, 1942.

———. Robert Frost. *The Years of Triumph,* 1915–1938. New York: Holt, Rinehart, and Winston, 1942.

Trilling, Lionel. "A Speech on Robert Frost: A Cultural Episode." *Partisan Review 26* (Summer 1959): 445–52.

Vander Ven, Tom. "Robert Frost's Dramatic Principle of 'Oversound.'" *American Literature* 45 (1973): 238–51.

Viereck, Peter. "Parnassus Divided." *Atlantic Monthly* 184 (October 1949): 67–70.

Vogt, Victor E. "Narrative and Drama in the Lyric: Robert Frost's Strategic Withdrawal." *Critical Inquiry 5* (1979): 529–51.

Warren, Robert Penn. "The Themes of Robert Frost." In *Selected Essays.* New York: Random House, 1958.

Winters, Yvor. "Robert Frost: Or, The Spiritual Drifter as Poet." *In The Function of Criticism.* Denver: Alan Swallow, 1957.

Index of
Themes and Ideas